The Second World War

The Second World War

A People's History

JOANNA BOURKE

OXFORD
UNIVERSITY PRESS

Great Clarendon Street, Oxford OX2 6DP

Oxford University Press is a department of the University of Oxford.
It furthers the University's objective of excellence in research, scholarship,
and education by publishing worldwide in

Oxford New York

Athens Auckland Bangkok Bogotá Buenos Aires Cape Town
Chennai Dar es Salaam Delhi Florence Hong Kong Istanbul Karachi
Kolkata Kuala Lumpur Madrid Melbourne Mexico City Mumbai Nairobi
Paris São Paulo Shanghai Singapore Taipei Tokyo Toronto Warsaw

with associated companies in Berlin Ibadan

Published in the United States
by Oxford University Press Inc., New York

British Library Cataloguing in Publication Data

Data available

Library of Congress Cataloging in Publication Data
Bourke, Joanna.
The Second World War : a people's history / Joanna Bourke.
Includes bibliographical references and index.
1. World War, 1939–1945 I. Title.
D743 .B62 2001   904.53—dc21   2001045152

ISBN 0–19–280224–0

1 3 5 7 9 10 8 6 4 2

Typeset in New Baskerville
by RefineCatch Limited, Bungay, Suffolk
Printed in Great Britain
on acid-free paper by
Biddles Ltd, Guildford and King's Lynn

Contents

CONTENTS

List of Figures

List of Maps

Introduction

No one has said that killing is easy. Yet, war depends upon large numbers of people being prepared to slaughter large numbers of other people. In the modern period, the Second World War took this commonplace military requirement to new depths. It left a devastated world in its wake. The map of the world had to be redrafted. Entire economies had been destroyed, but the psychological burden of mass human destruction was incalculable. For many people, the physical and psychological havoc was difficult to bear. As one young American infantryman stammered after stabbing to death a man with his bayonet: 'that bothered me ... my father taught me never to kill.'

The stark ugliness of combat escaped no one. The killers—mainly young men, but also many women, children, and the elderly—rarely avoided the feelings of panic, disgust, and despair that accompanied acts of grotesque brutality. The writer William Manchester recalled that, after killing a Japanese soldier in the Pacific, he cried 'I'm sorry' and started sobbing, before vomiting and urinating in his uniform. The victims too came from every age group, gender, class, and nationality. Some were executioners before they became victims. Terror was always a central component of this war. Military campaigns, strategy, and 'collateral damage' are important aspects of war, but injuring and destroying human beings is at the heart of military conflict. War involves killing people: the multiple ways in which this could be achieved were never so clearly demonstrated as during the Second World War.

Total War

The Second World War was the greatest cataclysm in modern history. This was truly a 'world war'. Just compare this conflict with its major predecessor. During the First World War, twenty-eight states participated in the bloodletting. Sixty-one states leapt at each other's throats between 1939 and 1945. The dedication of the entire globe to the waging of war and the breaking-down of distinctions between the battlefield and the home front were the chief traits of this conflict. Without question, the Second World War propelled the notion of 'total war' into dizzily horrifying heights. Indeed, civilians were the victims-of-choice. Again, this is most starkly brought out by a comparison with the First World War. While only 5 per cent of deaths in the 1914–18 war were civilian deaths, 66 per cent of deaths in the 1939–45 war were of civilians. Many more civilians than military personnel were killed in Belgium, China, France, Greece, Hungary, the Netherlands, Norway, Poland, the Soviet Union, and Yugoslavia. Furthermore, by whatever definition we use, large proportions of these victims were indisputably innocent. This book contains many examples of this frightening fact. The Holocaust is the pre-eminent instance of the wanton slaughter of non-combatants. But this was also the case in many other campaigns of the war. For example, of the six million Poles (Jews and non-Jews) who were killed by the Germans, one-third were children.

Finally, the Second World War deserves its reputation as the most horrifying event in modern history for the way in which processes of dehumanization and killing were founded upon so-called rational calculation. Science and technology were applied to the most murderous ends known to humankind. The range of uses was astounding, involving impersonal aerial bombardment, depersonalized murder in gas chambers, and face-to-face executions of entire communities. It is no wonder that, for the 85 million men and women who served (and survived) in one of the armed forces during the war and for the vast population of people caught up in the slaughter (and surviving), the war was the most unforgettable moment in their lives.

Confusion and complexity are the dominant characteristics of this 'total war'. For this reason, every history of the Second World War is necessarily fractured and incomplete. This is even more the case in a book of this brevity. Each participating nation tells a separate story of 'the war' and very few points of agreement can be found. Even such basic questions such as 'what', 'when', and 'who' are disputed. What is this military conflict called? For the British it is the Second World War, while the Americans call it World War Two; for the Russians it is the Great Patriotic War, while the Japanese designate it the Greater East Asia War. There is wide disagreement about the name of the most atrocious event of the war: the massacre of 6 million Jews. Should it be called the Holocaust, the Shoah, 'the Event', a genocide, an extermination, a mass murder, 'l'univers concentration-naire', or even the Nazi phrase, 'the Final Solution'? This book will use the word 'Holocaust', Greek for 'whole burn-ing' or 'burnt sacrifice to God'. But what do these words mean for the 14–16 million non-Jews who were also victims of Nazi mass murder? After all, Poles, Slavs, and Gypsies were also targeted for genocidal slaughter, and German Commun-ists, Jehovah Witnesses, 'asocial' criminals, mentally and physically handicapped, the chronically ill, and homosexuals were victims as well.

On a more prosaic level, when did the war begin? Some Japanese date it from 1931 (or *Shōwa 6*, according to the Japanese calendar), when their troops occupied Manchuria, a border province of China. This heralded what the Japa-nese call 'the dark valley' (or *kurai tanima*), a decade and a half of war. Britain, France, and the Commonwealth coun-tries date the war from September 1939, although the British public experienced a lengthy period of the 'phoney war' until April 1940. For the Russians, war really began in June 1941, despite the fact that the Red Army was already engaged in battle in Finland. The Americans got on board only in December 1941 (but their ships were implicated well before that date).

Also, of course, the enemy differed depending on which 'side' you were on—and that could change quite rapidly. Even within a single country, there may not be agreement on the nature of the enemy. For instance, a Pole in Lwow had good reasons to fear the Russians or Ukrainians, while a Pole in Warsaw was more liable to feel terrorized at the appearance of Germans. Americans on the East Coast might be slightly more anxious about the German threat, while West Coast residents were much more worried over Japan.

Finally, for millions of combatants and non-combatants alike, the greatest enemy did not possess a human face at all. 'Nature', with indiscriminate fury, could attack at any time. As one American private serving in Lorraine cursed: life was 'a goddam-muddy-field where a man's feet were always wet, a sonofabitch-of-a-sky that threatened rain, a pain-in-the-ass-of-a-woods from which a Heinie sniper could fire at us and stay hidden for hours'. In the war in Eastern Europe, the harsh climate competed successfully with artillery shells and bullets in killing people. The German soldier Bernhard Bechler described the situation he found himself just outside Stalingrad:

> Just imagine the scene: steppe, everything frozen, sub-zero temperatures of minus 20 or 30 degrees, masses of snow . . . German soldiers were lying on the ground and German tanks ran over these soldiers because they were no longer able to get up and make themselves known. I was thinking to myself, subconsciously: if people at home could see us here, if they could only see our soldiers dying so wretchedly![1]

Wherever you stood or crouched, there lurked an ugly and violent death.

Telling War Stories

Inevitably, this is neither an easy nor a pleasant story to tell. It is legitimate to ask why we even need another history—and a very short one at that—of the Second World War. It is impossible not to sympathize with some commentators who insist that it is *impossible* to speak about certain aspects of the war. In particular, they argue that even attempting to write about the terrors of the Holocaust implicates us vicariously in the horrors that were perpetrated. They are concerned that attempts to 'explain' the deeds of the perpetrators will render their actions 'understandable' and therefore 'forgivable'. The Holocaust is, and should be, literally unspeakable. The psychoanalyst and former Dachau prisoner Bruno Bettelheim put it succinctly: 'There are acts so vile that our task is to reject and prevent them, not to try to understand them.'

For commentators who believe that the Holocaust is literally 'unspeakable', no argument will change their mind, but I cannot embrace their silence. It is clear that the participants—victims as well as perpetrators—are impelled by the need to tell their stories, to communicate what happened, to search for a 'why', and to attempt to forge some kind of meaning out of the chaos that was their individual experience of the Holocaust. Today there is an even more pressing reason to speak and write about such events: a new generation is among us who possess little or no knowledge of this war. We are at risk of 'forgetting'. As the survivors gradually die, their memory is being overtaken by stories told by the victors and (most disturbingly) by 'Holocaust deniers'— powerful groups with their own extreme right-wing political agendas. There is also the threat that the translation of 'the war' into just another story of battles and strategies will dilute its horror. The sanitization of the war in some military histories is dangerous. Mass slaughter becomes a bland recital of 'body counts'. The anonymous enumeration of millions of men, women, and children killed or wounded, the numbing statistics estimating the proportion of cities destroyed, and the meaningless recital of the weight of various armaments can distance us from the victims. A similar process of dehumanization enabled atrocious behaviour to take place during the war. When Joseph Stalin (the dictator of the USSR) quipped that 'a single death is a tragedy, a million deaths is a statistic', he was drawing attention to a very frightening possibility. In the perhaps apocryphal words of the historian Simon Dubnov, just before he was killed by a Lithuanian policeman during the destruction of the Riga ghetto: 'Good people, do not forget, good people, tell your story.'[2] If this *People's History* errs in omitting too many strategic intricacies and technological advances in order to allow individual participants to tell us about their experiences, I hope that I will be excused. Admittedly, it would be ludicrous to imply that the individuals who appear in this book are in any way 'representative', 'typical', or even necessarily 'ordinary'. Nationality, gender, class, age, political beliefs, and so on single out these individuals from all others—but they serve to remind us of some of the people upon whom the brunt of the war fell. It is to be hoped that readers will be stimulated by this book to follow up their reading by looking at the mass of other material—written from different perspectives—that proliferates on library shelves.

2

The Declaration of War in Europe

A mere twenty years after the rivers of blood flowing from the First World War had been staunched, the European Powers embarked on further carnage. In 1918, people in all participating nations had united to recite the Hungarian slogan *nem, nem, soha!* ('no, no, never!'). Poets and novelists were at the forefront of this movement. After the First World War, politicians, religious leaders, and pacifists in all the warring nations had emphasized time and again the need to learn from the carnage between 1914 and 1918. In the words of the French pacifist Édouard Herriot, in a speech on 1 February 1925 appealing for money for a peace monument, 'It is we pacifists who are the most true to the teachings of the war.'[1] But the slaughter was to start anew, and the actual experience of this conflict was to deal a cruel blow to the high ideals of anti-war commentators throughout the world. How could this have happened?

Origins of the European War

No one agrees on the origins of the war in Europe. The desire to locate its beginnings in a single 'event' or 'tendency' has obscured the multifarious origins of this complex military conflict. There is also the question of how far back into history we must search for a cause. Many historians trace the origins of the Second World War to the earlier 'world war'. Indeed, they argue that the Second World War cannot be clearly distinguished from the First World War: what Europeans experienced was a 'Thirty Years War' of the twentieth century. We may not wish to go that far, but it is true that imposing the humiliating Treaty of Versailles (1919) on the defeated powers and forcing them to mortgage their economies with an outlandish reparations bill set up a marker for another major conflict. As one historian put it: 'Powers will be Powers.'[2] In other words, it was inevitable that Germany would seek to regain what it regarded as its rightful place in the world.

In Germany, the Treaty of Versailles was followed by rampant inflation and then, after a brief breathing space, by a severe economic depression: it was not unexpected that many Germans responded by looking back to the glorious days of the Wilhelmine Empire. But by 1938, under the Nazis, the economic outlook in Germany had changed. The economic recovery fuelled the sense of injustice that had arisen in the aftermath of the First World War. The strength of the German economy had resulted in a balance-of-payments crisis caused largely by the need to pay for the dramatic increase in imports of food and raw material. Industry and rearmament required ever more resources—

and Hitler's regime was increasingly looking outside Germany to meet these needs.

Furthermore, defeat in the First World War had failed to remove Germany's eastward ambitions. Adolf Hitler successfully played upon this national obsession. In this sense, Hitler's policy was fundamentally one of continuity with German politicians prior to 1918 and during the Weimar period. When Hitler came to power in 1933, National Socialism seemed to hold out the promise of a revived Germanic nation. Hitler did not invent many of the ideas that led to war. His promotion of the supposed need for *Lebensraum* (or 'living space') can be traced back to the nineteenth century, and his racist Social Darwinism was widely accepted by the early twentieth century in Germany. Finally, although Hitler's pathological hatred of the Jews is unquestioned (in *Mein Kampf* he called them subhumans, a cancer that had to be removed), the belief that Jews were responsible for all of Germany's ills—and particularly its fate during the First World War—was widely held by many Germans, on the hard and soft right, and originated in the rise of racial anti-Semitism in late Imperial Germany.

This emphasis on the ways Hitler epitomized wider concerns within German society in the 1930s can easily lead to a crude reductionism that employs a very simple equation: no Hitler, no war. It cannot be disputed that Hitler was a domineering political personality in Germany. It is difficult to imagine the Third Reich without him. He possessed a fanatical will and was at the same time an unprincipled opportunist. His desire to gain *Lebensraum* for his 'Aryan race' in Eastern Europe was wholehearted. As he wrote in *Mein Kampf*:

> To demand the borders of 1914 is political nonsense of such
> a degree and consequence that it appears a crime ... The
> borders of 1914 meant nothing to the German nation ... We
> National Socialists, by contrast, must without wavering keep
> to our foreign policy aim, which is to secure to the German
> nation the soil and space to which it is entitled on this earth.[3]

Nor is there disagreement about his willingness to impose his
will upon all his subordinates. When any of his subordinates,
like his first Foreign Minister, Konstantin von Neurath,
seemed reluctant to follow his lead into war, they were
replaced. However, it is far too easy to be carried away by this
image of the ultimate in human evil. Indeed, this image of
Hitler is largely a construction of Nazi as well as Allied
propaganda. It is dangerous to place too much emphasis
upon Hitler as a cause of the war—whether as a personality in
his own right or as someone who managed to epitomize
wider and more entrenched national desires and ideologies.
Much evidence suggests that Hitler had no coherent plan.
Certainly, he was willing to risk millions of his own people
in the pursuit of a racially 'pure', rejuvenated, Greater
Germany. But he was more likely simply to take advantage
of things as they happened, rather than working to a
pre-planned strategy. Too much of the explanation for the
origins of war has been placed on Hitler's lust for domination, and not enough on the expansionist ideology of
Nazism.

However, if focusing on Hitler is a form of reductionism, so
too is an excessive emphasis on ideology. Some historians
want to claim that the war grew out of a conflict of competing
ideologies. Totalitarianism in Germany, Italy, and Japan
faced up to the liberal democracies of Britain, France, and

the United States. According to this argument, the Axis countries—and Germany in particular—failed to develop a strong liberal-democratic tradition. In other words, the problem was not Hitler but Germany. Hitler's anti-Semitism, virulent nationalism, and antisocialism were simply more extreme than those shared by earlier German leaders and 'ordinary Germans'. This explanation is also unsatisfactory. The problem with blaming 'fascism' is that it fails to differentiate between the very different forms of this political ideology. Italian fascism was very distinctive from National Socialism, and neither resembled Japanese totalitarianism.

Finally, the origins of the war may also be traced to strategic concerns. War was inevitable if the territorial ambitions of certain nations were to have any hope of being achieved. Germany and Italy believed that they had something to gain from war. Hitler's plan vastly to expand the amount of land available for exploitation by the Aryan race in Eastern Europe has already been mentioned. The Italian dictator, Benito Mussolini, also pursued a foreign policy that was concerned with the supposed need for *spazio vitale* (again, 'living space') for Italians in North Africa and the Middle East. Mussolini's willingness to act upon this need was clearly signalled in October 1935, when Italian troops from neighbouring Italian Somililand and Eritrea invaded Abyssinia (modern-day Ethiopia). A year later, Italy and Germany militarily supported General Francisco Franco, the fascist dictator in Spain. Franco's victory in 1939 was a major economic as well as political coup for both powers. Spain's iron ore, tin, copper, zinc, and mercury were henceforth at their service. Mussolini also had ambitions of establishing Italy as one of the Great Powers. Thus, when Mussolini signed the Pact of Steel with Hitler in May 1939 (which committed Germany and Italy to support each other with all their military forces 'on land, sea, and in the air'), he signalled his desire dramatically to extend Italy's 'Roman' empire.

Strategically, the origin of the war was more complex for the Soviet Union. At first, Stalin pursued a defensive foreign policy. The Nazi–Soviet Non-Aggression Pact of August 1939 decreed that Russia would remain neutral should Germany attack Poland. For Stalin, it was an attempt to protect the Soviet Union from German aggression. Stalin signed the Pact only after his attempts to find agreement with Britain and France had been rebuffed. The Pact came as a surprise to the other Great Powers. After all (as Figure 1 illustrates), Hitler regarded the Russians as the 'scum of the earth', while Stalin viewed Hitler as the 'bloody assassin of the workers'. Whatever Stalin's long-term plans involved, it is clear that Hitler always intended the Pact to be a short-term strategy. In the words of the German ambassador to Italy, Ulrich von Hassell, in his diary of 29 August 1939:

> About the Russian pact Hitler said that he was in no wise altering his fundamental anti-bolshevist policies; one had to use Beelzebub to drive away the devil; all means were justified in dealing with the Soviets, even such a pact as this. This was a typical example of his conception of 'Realpolitik'.[4]

However, in the short term at least, the Pact proffered a great prize to the Soviet Union. The Pact had a secret clause dividing Poland between Germany and the Soviet Union. Stalin clearly understood that the Soviet Union needed to protect itself—and one way Stalin conceived of doing this was by creating a buffer zone.

1 'Rendezvous', showing Hitler meeting Stalin over the Nazi–Soviet Non-Aggression Pact (cartoon by David Low)

Appeasement

Even given the frustrations imposed by the Versailles Treaty, the personality of Hitler, the ideological imperative, and the territorial ambitions of the Axis nations, was a 'world war' inevitable? No, declare some historians, who blame British and French politicians for failing to stop German rearmament and for adopting a policy of appeasement. Accusatory fingers are pointed at the 'guilty men': Neville Chamberlain (the Conservative Prime Minister of Britain), Sir Samuel

Hoare (a Conservative British minister), Lord Halifax (the British Foreign Secretary), Pierre Laval (French Foreign Minister and Premier 1934–6), and Georges Bonnet (French Minister of Foreign Affairs 1938–9).

At the time, the arguments put forward by the appeasers could be convincing. No politician epitomized their views better than Chamberlain, the most despised of all British appeasers. In 1938, he explained his motives in language that may still strike a chord today. He reminded the nation of the war that had been concluded exactly twenty years earlier:

> When I think of those terrible four years and I think of the 7,000,000 of young men who were cut off in their prime, the 13,000,000 who were maimed and mutilated, the misery and the suffering of the mothers and the fathers, the sons and the daughters, and the relatives and the friends of those who were killed, and the wounded, then I am bound to say again what I have said before . . . in war, whichever side may call itself the victor, there are no winners, but all are losers. It is those thoughts which have made me feel that it was my prime duty to strain every nerve to avoid a repetition of the Great War in Europe.[5]

Was Chamberlain a weak politician incapable of understanding the perfidious nature of the threat facing Britain and the rest of Europe or did he have a realistic understanding of the military weakness of Britain and France? Were the appeasers cowards or cynical capitalists hoping to drive Germany into conflict with the Soviet Union? In other words, did the appeasers 'hope for the best but prepare for the worst' (as the historian A. J. P. Taylor put it) or did they prepare the way for the worst by ignoring better options? However we answer these questions, it is evident that, as late as December

1938, many people in Britain still believed that appeasement would work. Their hopes were bolstered by the infamous conference in Munich on 28 September 1938 where the leaders of Germany, Italy, Britain, and France agreed to the Sudetenland becoming part of the Third Reich. Later, Hitler signed a promise that Britain and Germany would 'never go to war with one another again'. This was the worthless 'piece of paper' that Chamberlain flourished upon his return to Britain. The attack on Czechoslovakia by Germany in March 1939 put an end to such hopes. On 15 March 1939, Czechoslovakia was dismembered; Bohemia and Moravia were made 'Protectorates'of Germany, Slovakia became an independent state, and Hungary occupied the province of Ruthenia. When the the non-German ethnic remnant of Czechoslovakia was conquered, the appeasers' belief that all Hitler wanted was to 'revise' Versailles by bringing ethnic Germans on the Reich borders into the Reich was shattered. If Czechoslovakia was to be overrun, what country was safe?

Whatever the other factors leading to the world war, German and Italian ambitions were crucial. In the beginning at least, Britain and France sought to satisfy them without war and without compromising too many of their own economic and political interests. Coping with Czechoslovakia had been difficult enough. But, following on the German invasion of Czechoslovakia, the British issued a guarantee to Poland that could not be broken so easily. Diplomacy crumbled irremediably on 1 September 1939 when German troops stormed into Poland and the *Luftwaffe* bombed Warsaw. Ten-year-old Janine Phillips, a young Polish boy, described the sense of horror and despair felt by his family the day Hitler invaded his country. His diary recorded their reactions:

Hitler has invaded Poland. We heard the bad news on the wireless a few minutes after spotting two aeroplanes circling around each other ... Everybody was stunned ... Grandpa turned the switch off and looked at our anguished faces. He knelt in front of the picture of Jesus Christ and started to pray aloud. We repeated after Grandpa, 'Our Father who art in Heaven, hallowed be Thy name ...'[6]

In Britain, Parliament erupted in fury. Even the appeasers were aghast. A meeting of the Cabinet confirmed everyone's fears: there was to be all-out war. On 3 September, Britain declared war and dragged the Dominions with it. Only Ireland remained neutral. A 9-year-old boy from Tyneside (England) remembered the announcement of war. Like Janine Phillips in Poland, he also heard it on a radio broadcast, but his prayers seemed to bounce down off the ceiling. 'Mr Chamberlain's broadcast was impressive,' he recalled:

I remembered him from the newsreels, coming out of his aeroplane after Munich, waving his little piece of paper and promising 'peace in our time'. I thought he looked like a sheep, and now he bleated like a sheep. He talked about notes being sent and replies not being received. He *regretted* that a state of war now existed between Great Britain and Germany. He sounded really *hurt*, like Hitler was some shift-less council tenant who had failed to pay his rent after faith-fully promising to do so ... The sirens went immediately. We didn't know what to do ... I couldn't stand still—I went into my bedroom and considered trying to pray, a thing I hadn't done for years. It didn't seem much use against Nazi bombers.[7]

The second worldwide war of the century had begun in

Europe, and children were caught in the middle of it all. While iconoclastic images of the First World War involve mud-splattered soldiers in trenches, the central images of the Second World War were to be of children: the London child wandering, dazed, through the ruins of the East End in 1940, or the cloth-capped child holding his hands up at gunpoint in the Warsaw ghetto, or even the line of child recruits being inspected by a morose Hitler near the end of the war. In 1939, however, no one could predict the full extent of the horror to come.

America, Japan, and the European War

America did not follow the lead of Britain. In the 1930s, American politics were characterized by isolationism in foreign policy and a preoccupation with internal affairs. This desire to remain aloof from Europe's quarrels had grown out of disillusionment arising from the First World War. In 1934-5, a congressional committee (known as the Nye Committee) focused on American participation in the First World War, concluding that American intervention had been profoundly influenced by bankers and munitions exporters—in other words, by those who stood to profit from American participation in a foreign war. The Nye Report coincided with widespread public disquiet about the huge loss of lives of American soldiers in the 1917–18 war. Between 1935 and 1937, Congress had passed a series of neutrality acts in an attempt to ensure that America was not sucked into war. This legislation was generally well accepted: the 'America First' movement was strong. The presidential race of 1940, where Franklin D. Roosevelt stood for a third time, was vicious, with his opponents claiming that he harboured un-American, dictatorial propensities and would 'plow under every fourth American boy', while Roosevelt promised that 'Your boys are not going to be sent into any foreign wars'.

In addition, most Americans did not perceive Hitler to be an immediate threat to the United States, and, while Japan was clearly a threat to the Far East, it was thought to be too dependent upon American oil, gasoline, and scrap iron to be worth worrying about. Thus, American policy was cautious, anxious not to provoke attack. This changed in November 1938 when the Japanese Prime Minister proclaimed a 'New Order in East Asia'. America rightly saw this as an attack on China and, by early 1940, had enforced a trade embargo. When Japan stationed troops in northern Indochina, Roosevelt moved the Pacific Fleet from the West Coast to Pearl Harbor, to guard against any further advance of Japan eastwards. By this time, there were concerns about the negative impact that a Europe under Hitler would have upon American economic interests. Aware that it was crucial that Hitler was defeated, Roosevelt found ways to support the European war. Nevertheless, it was only in late 1939 that Congress finally repealed the prohibition on the export of arms. Even then, it insisted that the purchasing nations collect the arms themselves—the infamous 'cash and carry principle'. Since British ships had to be protected as they delivered the goods, American warships were sent into the Atlantic on patrol. Roosevelt also supported Britain through the 'lend-lease' accord, whereby America would lend or lease food and weapons to Britain on condition that they were returned after the war. This was war by proxy and was eventually to cost America $50 billion.

The first major indication that Japan had become an unacceptable threat to America and that both countries would contribute to the European war came on 27 September 1940, when the Tripartite Pact between Japan, Germany, and Italy was signed. From Germany's point of view, this was an appropriate time for such a pact. As we shall see in the next chapter, by this stage Italy was completely dependent upon Germany, and Germany's victory in the Netherlands and France had opened up colonial territories in Asia. For Japan, there were also good reasons for the Pact. Japan was already involved in a particularly bloody war with China. America's oil embargo was a bitter blow to Japanese ambitions. As a consequence, Japan seemed to have nothing to lose by bombing Pearl Harbor on the island of Oahu, Hawaii.

The Japanese attack on Pearl Harbor was the most dramatic example of a surprise attack during the war. The scale of the operation was immense: six fleet carriers of the Japanese Imperial Navy, transporting 430 aircraft, were involved. It was not only Pearl Harbor that suddenly found itself in the midst of battle: so too did the Philippines, Singapore, Malaya, Thailand, Bangkok, Guam, Wake Island, and Hong Kong (these campaigns are the subject of another chapter). The attack was planned by the Commander-in-Chief of the Combined Fleet, Admiral Isoroku Yamamoto. He was aware of America's strength and wrote that, if war was to come, he would be able to 'run wild for the first six months or a year, but I have no confidence for the second and third years'.[8]

On the 7 December 1941, 183 aircraft took off towards Hawaii. Mismanagement and failure in communications meant that the half-hour warning that the Japanese had intended did not happen. The result was total surprise. American personnel were unable to retaliate effectively: nothing could be done to protect themselves from the torrent of bombs. Even those American servicemen who managed to escape the thick fires on their ships were mercilessly strafed in the water and on the ground by diving planes. Within two hours, Japanese aircraft had destroyed all except 79 of the 231 American aircraft, 7 of the 8 battleships were severely damaged, and 2,403 American personnel had been killed, with another 1,178 wounded. America's Pacific Fleet had shown itself to be vulnerable, lined up like 'ducks in a shooting gallery', as one Japanese pilot put it.

Pearl Harbor caused national fury in the United States. Many Americans regarded the attack as an example of dastardly behaviour on the part of the Japanese, who had not declared war. Roosevelt echoed the sentiments of most Americans when he declared, in Congress the following day, that 7 December 1941 was 'a date that will live in infamy'. On 8 December 1941, Roosevelt asked Congress to recognize that a state of war existed between the USA and Japan. Even then, Roosevelt did not ask Congress to declare war on Germany, but waited until 11 December, when Hitler declared war on the USA. The 'isolationists' who had lobbied tirelessly on the theme that Americans should never involve themselves in European conflicts were decisively silenced. Conspiracy theories abounded, however (and continue to be believed by some). According to the conspiratory theorists, a cabal of officials, including Roosevelt, Cordell Hull, Henry Stimson, Frank Knox, and George Marshall, had deliberately lured the Japanese into attacking America so as to find an excuse for American participation. Some historians have suggested that Roosevelt had known of the forthcoming attack on Pearl Harbor and had allowed it to take place without warning in order to find an excuse for bringing the USA into the war. They draw attention to the fact that all of the US carriers 'just happened' to be at sea that day rather than in their usual berths at Pearl Harbor and that, while drawing up the Atlantic Charter (which enunciated war aims) in Newfoundland, Roosevelt had told Churchill that 'Everything was to be done to force an "incident" that would lead to war.' A milder version claims, at the very least, that Roosevelt and Churchill were aware of the forthcoming attack and refrained from sending out a warning in order to propel America into the war. In reality, however, there is no evidence for these claims, even if it may be true that Roosevelt was relieved that America could now enter the war fully.

The bombing made Americans aware that security was now a global consideration. After all, if Japan could attack Pearl Harbor, the USA had to extend its security web across the Pacific. The vast spread of ocean was no longer sufficient protection. As Roosevelt argued in his 'fireside chat' of 23 February 1942, it was no longer wise for 'the American eagle to imitate the tactics of the ostrich'. War was global and the American eagle had to 'fly high and strike hard'.

The American eagle was not in a particularly strong position. There was legitimate concern about the military capability of America at this time. As late as May 1941, America possessed only one combat-ready division, compared with Germany's 208 and Japanese's 100-plus. The USA had fewer than 500 military aircraft and 200 tanks, while the Germans had 2,700 military aircraft and 3,500 tanks on the Eastern Front alone. Nevertheless, American industry rallied to the call and within one year of declaring war was producing 4,000 military aircraft a month. This had doubled by 1944. There was a massive growth in the US military machine. In 1939, America spent only $1.3 billion on the military. By 1945, this had risen to $80.5 billion. By 1944, America was producing 40 per cent of the world's armaments and 60 per cent of combat munitions used by the Allies.

In Japan, the bombing of Pearl Harbor was greeted with joy. After all, a lot was at stake for the Japanese. For them, negotiating a New Order with America was crucial if they were to control the land and islands stretching from Burma to the central Pacific, an area including half of the world's population. The nihilist writer Dazai Osamu described how 'my whole personality suddenly changed. I felt invisible rays piercing through my body, and holy spirits wafting around me. ... A new Japan was born on that morning.'[9] Most Japanese civilians concurred. The recollections of Itabashi Kôshû were fairly typical. He recalled:

> I was in the second year of middle school that day, Pearl Harbor Day. 'Well, we really did it!' I thought. The sound of the announcement on the radio still reverberates in my ears ... 'News special, News special,' high pitched and rapid. 'Beginning this morning before dawn, war has been joined with the Americans and British.' I felt as if my blood boiled and my flesh quivered. The whole nation bubbled over, excited and inspired. 'We really did it! Incredible! Wonderful!' That's the way it felt then.[10]

Thus, twenty-eight months after Britain and the dominions had declared war, America joined in the fray. America's declaration of war was formally made on 7 December 1941 and a few days later—on 11 December—Hitler and Mussolini followed suit, also declaring war on the United States. Meanwhile, terror had struck in Europe.

3

Occupied Europe

litzkrieg! The word sends a shudder through the body of any veteran of the Second World War. It signalled an unprecedented use of military force, combining the brutal application of technological might with lightning speed. In a Blitzkrieg ('lightning war'), Tiger or Panzer tanks, with the support of Stuka dive-bombers from the Luftwaffe, moved quickly across territory, leaving destruction in their wake. Without question, German ascendancy in Western Europe was heavily dependent upon new ways of using military hardware, particularly air power. It was the aeroplane that transformed the Second World War into 'total war'. During the First World War, the aeroplane had limited (albeit still terrifying) uses. The first major hint of the power of the flying machine in destroying masses of people came with the bombing of Guernica during the Spanish Civil War of 1936–9. This conflict reinforced two main ideas. First, it showed that the aeroplane could be used to quicken the pace of war, thus avoiding the stagnant trench warfare of the First World War by striking 'over and beyond' the war zone at the industrial bases supporting the troops. Secondly, it illustrated the ease and effectiveness with which civilians could become the chief victims of war. At the very beginning of the war—on the day that Poland was invaded—the American President, Roosevelt, appealed to all the warring countries not to target undefended towns and civilians: Britain, France, and (after a pause) Germany accepted this limitation. No one honoured these good intentions. From the first day of the Second World War until the last hour, the sinister hum of aeroplanes could be heard in the sky. Admittedly, planes were never capable of winning the war on their own. But command of the air was crucial to conquest on the ground.

Hitler's army and air force conquered Europe with a rapidity that was dizzying. Poland fell, followed, after a 'phoney war' lasting several months, by Belgium, Denmark, the Netherlands, and France. How should these populations have dealt with German occupation? Where did resignation end and collaboration begin? To what extent was individual, familial, and national survival dependent upon currying favour with the new masters of Europe? These were some of the difficult questions facing millions of people in the occupied territories.

Crushing Poland

On 1 September, German forces overran Poland. The wide, open plains of Poland were ideally suited to the rapid movement of tanks central to a blitzkrieg attack. The Polish Air Force was put out of action almost immediately—its small force of 350 combat aircraft was no match for its German counterpart. The 2,000 planes that bombed Warsaw (the capital city of Poland) launched the first indiscriminate bombing of a city in the war. It was not to be the last. Figure 2 shows the human cost of the invasion. The Germans proved expert in carrying through another strategic initiative when they landed troops by parachute, glider, and aeroplane. This was the first full-scale use of blitzkrieg. The Germans conquered everything in their path, enabling the Red Army to move forward on 17 September to claim its share of Poland, as promised by the secret clause in the Nazi–Soviet Non-Aggression Pact signed one month earlier. Although international law designated this Soviet move as an act of aggression, the Soviets protested that they were merely intervening because the Polish state had collapsed.

The rapidity of the German victory shocked the Allies. It had taken only one month to crush Poland. By 28 September, Poland had been partitioned, with the Russians grabbing 77,000 square miles and the remaining 73,000 square miles being placed under the 'protection' of the German Reich. Thus, between 17 September 1939 and 22 June 1941, the beautiful rivers of Narew, Vistula, and San divided Poland between the two occupying countries of Germany and the Soviet Union. Prior to the occupation, Hitler had admitted that 'the destruction of Poland is our primary task. The aim is not the arrival at a certain line but the annihilation of living forces.' He advised his men to 'Be merciless. Be brutal. It is necessary to proceed with maximum severity. The war is to be a war of annihilation.'[1] German soldiers were willing to obey, sharing Hitler's characterization of the Poles. Their diaries are replete with disparaging references to 'Polacks', 'primitive peoples', and the 'animal sub-humanity of the Poles'.[2]

As a consequence, it is little wonder that terror was an

2 Polish girl weeping over her sister, killed by German bombing of
Poland

integral part of the occupation. Just one statistic can illustrate the level of brutality endured by the Poles during the war: around 20 per cent of the population of Poland was killed, compared with less than 2 per cent of the French population while they were occupied by Axis powers. In order to weaken Polish resistance, the SS targeted the intelligentsia: teachers, writers, and the educated classes were particularly vulnerable. Children were also victimized. The Germans deported around 15 per cent of all Polish children as slaves to Germany. Of the 200,000 children taken, only 20,000 returned to Poland after the war. Children remaining in Poland were victims in other ways. As Heinrich Himmler decreed in his memorandum 'The Treatment of Racial Aliens in the East' of 25 May 1940, Polish children were not to be educated higher than the fourth grade of elementary school. In his words: 'The sole goal of this schooling is to teach them simple arithmetic, nothing above the number 500; writing one's name; and the doctrine that it is divine law to obey the Germans. . . . I do not think that reading is desirable.'[3]

In their quest for racial superiority, Germans murdered the inmates of mental institutions and tuberculosis sanatoria and herded the Jews into 'ghettos' in the cities, killing many and forcing the rest to live in conditions so bad that death rates soon began to soar.

Finally, national treasures were looted during the war. In just three months between December 1939 and March 1940, 100 libraries, 96 manors, 74 palaces, 43 historic churches, 15 museums, and innumerable art galleries were looted and the bounty carefully packed and sent to Germany. As late as 1990, the Polish government established a new post of Commissioner for Cultural Heritage Abroad to trace 'cultural losses' from the war.

In the Soviet part of Poland, the destruction may have been even more devastating, at least prior to 1941. While the Germans killed around 120,000 Poles between 1939 and 1941, the Russians killed more than 400,000. The graves of 25,700 Polish officers, soldiers, and civilians captured by the Red Army and massacred in April and May 1940 were later unearthed in the Katyn and Miednoje forests and in a wooded area on the outskirts of Kharkov. These were some of the earliest mass shootings of POWs during the war. In addition, over 1.2 million Poles, Jews, ethnic Volga Germans, Ukrainians, and Belorussians were forcibly deported to Siberia, the steppes of Kazakhstan, and remote regions in the Far East and north during these years. Their property was confiscated. Stalin set out ruthlessly to eradicate all signs and symbols of Polish identity. Repression became central to everyday life. Pettiness ruled. Poles were forbidden to ride in taxis, wear felt hats, walk in public parks, and carry briefcases. Everything recognizably Polish was banned, including Mass and the teaching of Polish history in schools. Polish was relegated to the status of a secondary language. A terrifying silence was imposed, as parents instructed their children to 'say nothing at school, speak to nobody, answer no questions, or else we go to Siberia'. Poland sank into a period named 'The Great Silence'.

Meanwhile, the Red Army invaded Finland, which had also been assigned to the USSR under the Nazi–Soviet Non-Aggression Pact of August 1939. The Soviets had expected a short war that would result in the establishment of a puppet government (the Terijoki Government) in Helsinki as the new 'Democratic Republic of Finland'. Between 30 November 1939 and March 1940, a one-million-strong Red Army clashed with 200,000 Finnish troops. The Soviet troops were not trained for deep-snow conditions, they had poor radio communications, and the long nights and heavy snow limited the support of Soviet aviation. In contrast, the Finns excelled at small-unit tactics in the forests, leaving the Soviet troops to stumble along the roads. This became known as the 'Winter War'. By March, Stalin had been forced to concede a humiliating defeat. The final agreement was not wholly in Finland's favour, however, since Finland was forced to cede 10 per cent of its territory to the USSR. The campaign was to have one crucial long-term impact: it gave the Germans a false image of the Red Army as a weak force, thus paving the way to 'Barbarossa', or the invasion of the Soviet Union by the Germans.

The Fall of France and Dunkirk

With Poland conquered, Hitler's armies felt confident enough to turn towards the west. By early April 1940, Denmark had been overrun, allowing Germany to dominate the Baltic and providing a site for German fighter planes. The Netherlands surrendered a month later, but not before the city of Rotterdam had been bombed, resulting in the death of around 1,000 civilians. The Dutch had proved too dependent upon defensive measures—particularly flooding—and had not taken into consideration the possibilities of war from the air. Norway was next to be attacked:

Hitler feared that the western Allies might use Norway to threaten Germany's northern flank. It quickly capitulated.

Meanwhile, France itself was subjected to a blitzkrieg. The declaration of war initially found France relatively calm. The American ambassador reported that mobilization for war was carried out

> in absolute quiet. The men left in silence. There were no bands, no songs. There were no shouts of 'On to Berlin' and 'Down with Hitler' to match the shouts of 'On to Berlin' and 'Down with the Kaiser!' as in 1914. There was no hysterical weeping of mothers and sisters and children. The self-control and quiet courage has been so far beyond the usual state of the human race that it has a dream quality.[4]

There was no premonition of the disaster to come.

To everyone's surprise, the French forces were rapidly routed. The technological superiority of the Germans and, more importantly, their superior tactics dealt France a crushing blow. Allied military leaders had lamentably failed to develop a strategy appropriate to the new way the Germans were conducting battle. The Allied forces failed to ensure adequate air–ground support and their combined arms tactics were deficient. Most importantly, they had not realized the strategic implications of speed in modern, technologically driven combat. The Germans excelled at fast warfare and French and British forces could not keep up. Within only six weeks, the French army had collapsed and shell-shocked Parisians were forced to watch as German soldiers paraded through their streets, the sound of their jackboots signalling the defeat of a great power. General Charles de Gaulle's famous prediction that the French had lost the battle but not the war never seemed more ludicrously optimistic than at this moment.

Not everything had gone Germany's way, however. At a crucial point, Hitler's armies paused. Keen to fly the swastika over Paris, Hitler ordered his tanks and troops to halt only fifteen miles from Dunkirk, enabling the 350,000 Allied troops trapped by the rapid German advance in the Dunkirk and Ostend area to escape. The Allies had understood at least one thing better than the Germans: the sea could be a highway, as much as a barrier. From 26 May, forty British, French, Belgian, and Dutch destroyers, accompanied later by around 900 privately owned craft (including Thames barges, pleasure steamers, and fishing boats), ferried the trapped troops to the safety of Britain. By 4 June, 350,000 men (one-third of whom were French) had been rescued. When the German troops became aware of the evacuation, they attempted to respond, but their efforts were impeded by poor weather, which grounded much of the *Luftwaffe*. All they could do was watch their enemies slipping away. It was after the Dunkirk evacuation that Winston Churchill (Britain's new Prime Minister) made his most famous speech in the House of Commons. On 4 June, Churchill declared: 'We shall fight on the beaches, we shall fight on the landing-grounds, we shall fight in the fields and in the streets, we shall fight in the hills; we shall never surrender.' But British triumphalism at the successful evacuation was soured by three facts: much of the troops' hardware had been left on the beaches; six British destroyers had been wrecked and another nineteen damaged; and, finally, Holland, Belgium, and soon a large part of France were under German occupation (see Map 1). France was left defenceless.

Map legend:

- The German Reich on 22 June 1941, the day of the German invasion of Russia
- Countries under German rule or influence by June 1941
- Neutral countries
- Great Britain, the only state at war with Germany on 21 June 1941; and the Soviet Union, to whom Britain immediately offered all possible help and alliance in the fight against Nazism

1 Europe, 22 June 1941

The human cost of Dunkirk was also high. From Britain's safe shores, what was happening at Dunkirk was difficult to comprehend. Denise Levertov had been evacuated to Buckinghamshire, where a faint sound of the battle could be heard. In her poem 'Listening to Distant Guns' she wrote:

> That low pulsation in the east is war:
> No bell now breaks the evening's silent dream.
> The bloodless clarity of evening's sky
> Betrays no whisper of the battle-scream.[5]

However, the men in Dunkirk had uttered battle screams and moans. Whenever the weather had cleared, dive-bombers of the *Luftwaffe* had attacked the helpless men. Many had gone crazy with terror. Others had mobbed the boats, causing them to capsize and drowning their wounded comrades. Fear had caused discipline to falter.

This aspect of Dunkirk is often forgotten. Instead, the 'glory of Dunkirk' became a symbol as much as an event and, as a consequence, its history is riddled with myth and nationalist bias. The contribution of the 'little men'—the independent fishermen and weekend sailors who contributed to the evacuation—has been exaggerated. After all, it was only in the last two days of the evacuation that the armada of civilian boats came to the rescue of the encircled armies. National pride has also played a large part in the story of Dunkirk. French historians imply that the British troops were fleeing through cowardice, while British historians blame the French for making evacuation necessary in the first place. However, although even Churchill described the evacuation as a 'deliverance' rather than a 'victory', it came to represent an important component of British national mythology. Morale was certainly bolstered by the events of those days and the 'Dunkirk Spirit' was to be called up many times in the following years, particularly during the bombing of Britain. Yet the fact was that British armed forces had suffered a resounding defeat.

The Battle of Britain

For Britain, the period of the 'phoney war' ended four months after Dunkirk. Initially, the bombing of British cities was a mistake. Prior to September 1940, the *Luftwaffe* had concentrated their attacks on coastal targets in Britain and on shipping. However, on 23 August 1940, the *Luftwaffe* accidentally dropped some bombs over London. In retaliation, the Royal Air Force (RAF) bombed Berlin. Hitler was furious and ordered attacks to commence on London.

The Battle of Britain lasted just eighty-two days, between 10 July and 31 October 1940. These were the days in which 'Death holds high festival', as the poet Mary Désirée Anderson put it in 'Blitz'. In the early days, the bombing was relentless. From 7 September to 13 November, London was bombed almost every day and every night. A young girl from the East End of London described the eerie feeling of being bombed:

> I remember racing towards the house, E pulling me and yelling. The oddest feeling in the air all around, as if the whole air was falling apart, quite silently. And then suddenly I was on my face, just inside the kitchen door. There seemed to be waves buffeting me, one after another, like bathing in a rough sea. I remember clutching the floor, the carpet, to prevent myself

being swept away. This smell of carpet in my nose and trying not to be swept away, and I could hear Mrs R screaming. E was nowhere, the lights were gone, it was all dust, I didn't even wonder if he was all right . . . didn't give him a thought.[6]

Glasgow, Belfast, Liverpool, Cardiff, Coventry, Bristol, Portsmouth, and Southampton were to suffer next. In the period to May 1941, 43,000 people were killed and another 1.5 million families made homeless. Half of the civilians killed were women. Indeed, by September 1942, the death rate of British civilians exceeded that of British soldiers. This remained the case until D-Day in 1944. In the end, however, the losses suffered by the *Luftwaffe* were crippling. During the Battle of Britain, the German air force lost 1,733 aircraft and 3,089 crew compared with 915 aircraft and 503 pilots within the RAF. As one commentator noted, 'London burned, but Britain was saved.'

Occupation

While Britain was bombed, France was in the process of being torn apart. On 10 July 1940, the Senators and Deputies voted by an overwhelming majority of 569 to 80 to give 84-year-old Marshal Henri Philippe Pétain full executive powers. Their vote signalled the decisive defeat of the Third Republic. Parliamentary democracy was no more: it was replaced by one of the most authoritarian regimes of twentieth-century Europe. A new government was formed under Pétain, who immediately asked the Germans for an armistice while calling on the French to lay down their arms. To make their victory even sweeter, the Germans insisted that the armistice be signed in the same railway carriage in which the Germans had acknowledged defeat on 11 November 1918. A bitter period of French history was inaugurated. On 24 October 1940, the term 'collaboration' was given its modern definition when Pétain met Adolf Hitler and agreed to cooperate. Photographs of the two men shaking hands were widely published.

The implications of the French surrender rapidly became clear. France was immediately divided into two zones. The Germans occupied Paris and the surrounding area, while French collaborationists governed the second zone from Vichy, a spa town in central France. How could this have happened? A main reason was that in the early days of the invasion the cult of the Marshal was strong. Pétain was trusted; he seemed to embody common sense and reasonableness in the face of the tragedy. At his side was the more flamboyant, arch-appeaser Pierre Laval. Together, they set about reconstructing a French nation that could coexist with Germany. Both saw collaboration as a necessity, not an option. It took two years before this basic political arrangement was to be reformed again. On 11 November 1942, the Germans (frightened by the Allied landings in North Africa) occupied all of France.

Persecution of the Jews

Persecution—along with its handmaiden, collaboration—began immediately after the defeat. Between 1940 and 1942, collaboration was the norm, not the exception. To the horror of the Allies, the policies of Aryanization and anti-Semitism adopted were not forced upon the French by Nazi pressure but were home-grown. In both occupied France and the unoccupied zone, anti-Jewish laws were enforced zealously. The Vichy government passed 143 laws and *actes reglementaires* against Jews. As early as 3 October 1940, Vichy promulgated the first statute on the Jews, without any German pressure. This statute excluded Jews from public office and set a limit on their numbers in the professions. The law was extended on 2 June 1941 and on 22 July 1941 in an attempt to 'eliminate all Jewish influence from the national economy'.

Then the Jews began to be rounded up. On 4 October 1940, foreign Jews (mainly from Eastern Europe or refugees from Germany and Austria) were placed in camps. From October 1940, all Jews had to register their name, profession, nationality, and address at their local police station. The census (or, more correctly, the death file) was called the Tulard dossier after Andre Tulard, the French civil servant in charge of the operation. By May 1942, all Jews in the occupied zone had to wear a yellow star. In July 1942, mass arrests began. The first 27,388 people arrested were chosen from the Tulard dossier. Contrary to common assumption, these arrests were not carried out by Germans: only Frenchmen took part in rounding up these Jews. Initially, at least, sharp distinctions were made between French Jews and foreign Jews, who constituted one-half of all Jews in France in 1940. Put bluntly, the Vichy government participated in the Final Solution, agreeing to hand over foreign Jews. The only other unoccupied territory that voluntarily did this was Bulgaria. In fact, French politicians and officials attempted to manipulate Nazi policy to rid France of foreign Jews. Later, when the

Germans began the mass deportations of Jews to death camps, the Vichy government even provided police support. It was only from the spring of 1943 that the German police took charge of these round-ups. It was this persecution of the French Jews between 1940 and 1942 (the date when Germany occupied all of France) that facilitated the Nazi deportation of 75,000 Jews to the death camps between 1942 and 1944. Of the 75,000 French Jews who were deported, only 4 per cent returned. Most of the others perished in the gas ovens, but a large proportion also died from disease, hard work, lack of food, and inadequate shelter.

Resistance in Western Europe

Civilians trapped in the occupied countries were often unsure of how to respond to their predicament. Many turned a blind eye to the atrocious activities of the occupiers, but the majority of men and women felt confused, demoralized, and unsure how they were expected to act. With astonishing speed, they became hardened to violence.

However, collaboration with fascism was not inevitable. Moral agency is crucial to what it means to be human. After all, the Nazis did not have a 'free hand' and their efforts were impeded by people's views of right and wrong. For instance, while the German Catholic Church did not oppose the transport of Jews, it did eventually oppose the mass murder of the handicapped. In fascist Italy, even under German occupation, anti-Semitic laws were not generally enforced. People were never, in practice, 'banal actors devoid of moral conscience' (Hannah Arendt's famous phrase).

This said, resistance was never easy, although there were innumerable gradations of risk. Symbolic resistance was understandably the most common form of resisting enemy occupation. Retired people pottered about in their gardens, planting flowers in the national colours. Workers would fasten paper clips to their collars ('we will stick together'), and adolescents would daub slogans in public toilets (as one Channel Islander admitted, subversive graffiti were 'How you got your kicks. These days they'd call you hooligans').[7] In occupied France, people would wear a black tie or ribbon on 14 June, the anniversary of the entry of the *Wehrmacht* into Paris. On Bastille Day, there would be a sartorial epidemic of clothes coloured red, white, and blue. In many countries, simply greeting Jewish neighbours in the street was risky enough.

More active forms of resistance included striking and assisting people 'on the run'. For instance, the Dutch went on strike in February 1941 over the persecution of the Jews, in spring 1943 when Dutch soldiers were sent to prisoner-of-war camps in Germany, and in September 1944 when Allied troops landed. Further, the Dutch underground hid around 25,000 Jews, of whom 6,000 remained undetected. Sabotage, intelligence, and armed revolt were even more dangerous. Such activity was encouraged by organizations such as the Special Operations Executive (SOE) in Britain and the Office of Strategic Services (OSS) in America. They were 'The Fourth Arm' in the war, after war by land, air, and sea, and they aimed to 'set Europe ablaze' (in Churchill's words) by working with other resistance groups. By the end of the war over 13,000 men and women had served in the SOE, and the OSS employed 13,000 people at its height in late 1944.

Generally, the greater the individual and group threat, the greater the resistance. Thus, in the occupied areas of the Soviet Union, Poland, and the Balkans, people had little to lose by resisting, since death was staring them in the face irrespective of their actions. In other occupied countries—such as in the Channel Islands, the only British territory to be occupied by the Germans during the war, and in the Netherlands, peopled with so-called Aryans—the relatively gentle nature of the occupation reduced much of the incentive for aggressive resistance, at least initially. The Channel Islanders were also subdued by the overwhelming presence of German troops (there was one German soldier to every two islanders). It was easier to resist when the Germans were thinner on the ground. Resistance was also influenced by geography. The flat, cleared landscape of the Channel Islands and Denmark militated against the roving bands of guerrillas that were so effective in mountainous countries like Greece and Italy. In many countries, the resistance had difficulty persuading rural people to support their cause. Peasant families in places like France often found their status and material well-being improved by German occupation, while partisan groups were ignorant of rural needs. Partisans would descend upon a village, consume vital foodstuffs, and leave at the slightest sign of trouble, leaving the villagers to suffer the murderous wrath of German troops. Only when the occupying troops proved more vicious than the partisans did rural communities support the resistance.

In many occupied countries, widespread resistance was only sparked off by threats of labour conscription. In the south of France, for instance, the *maquis* began with men fleeing into the hills to avoid being conscripted to work in factories. The Dutch and Norwegian resistance against the labour drafts was even more effective. In the Netherlands, massive labour strikes proved to be effective ways of resisting labour conscription. By mid-July, only 7 per cent of the men who had been conscripted had appeared for work. Similarly, in Norway, the 'boys in the forest' became a byword for resistance after the attempted labour mobilization of May 1944.

Women were crucial to many forms of resistance. They were involved in some of the most dangerous actions and many brave women SOE agents parachuted into occupied France; but more important were the larger group of women who were responsible for hiding escaping POWs, Jews, and other people at risk. Hiding the Jews in particular was an important way women resisted the Nazis in occupied Europe. The Belgians and the Dutch were particularly effective in this—although the Dutch became notorious for their most celebrated failure to protect the young Jewish girl Anne Frank, author of a subsequently famous diary, from deportation to the camps. This work was carried out by women such as the young Andrée De Jongh, whose escape network (called Comète) enabled over 700 Allied servicemen to escape from occupied Belgium. Without question, women were more 'invisible' than men in public places and were less likely to be regarded suspiciously by guards, police, secret agents, and troops.

Resisters emerged from the full range of political parties. Inevitably, Communists eventually were at the vanguard of resistance movements, despite their hesitant start owing to the invidious position they found themselves in after the Nazi–Soviet Non-Aggression Pact of 1939. Freed from this

Pact in June 1941 when the Germans attacked the Soviet Union, they rapidly made up for lost time, even to the extent of making alliances with their former enemies, the Catholics. However, resistance should not be regarded as innately revolutionary. In some countries, resistance took the form of fighting for the restoration of an old, aristocratic order. In Germany, resistance was muted and difficult. Up to the war, resistance had been mainly on the Left. By 1944, however, conservative military officers had taken the lead. Claus von Stauffenberg, a German war hero, was responsible in July 1944 for one of the two major bomb attempts on Hitler's life. He noted that 'We must commit high treason with all the means at our disposal.'[8] Hitler was wounded only slightly, because at the moment of the explosion he coincidentally leaned over a heavy wooden table. The conspirators were arrested and hanged slowly by piano wire. The small number of German resisters were as likely to be inspired by reactionary elitism as by a vision of a new, democratic Germany. The moral stance taken by German groups such as the White Rose, established by Hans and Sophie Scholl, was exceptional. In their most famous act of resistance, they dropped anti-Nazi leaflets into the main lobby of Munich University. The leaders, all aged between 22 and 25 years of age, were beheaded.

The wide political diversity in the resistance proved extremely problematical. Take the example of French resistance. General Charles de Gaulle, a French military Commander, had an immense impact. While in exile in London, he led the Free France resistance movement. His most famous speech was broadcast on 18 June 1940, when he claimed that 'whatever happens, the flame of French

Resistance must not and will not be extinguished'. The prophecy would take time to be realized, however. It was not until the German invasion of the USSR on 22 June 1941 that the French Communist Party took over the scattered remnants of French resistance, giving it form, organization, and the 'fire' of the sort called for by de Gaulle from his safe haven in London. However, French resistance movements remained highly divided on political grounds—that is, until May 1943, when Jean Moulin (sent by de Gaulle) managed to unite the leftists, unionists, and centrists into the Conseil Nationale de la Resistance. One of their most important actions was to declare their faith in de Gaulle, an action that was to have huge implications for de Gaulle's negotiations with the Allies. Meanwhile, the Communist Party coordinated a complex series of acts of sabotage and other forms of guerrilla warfare. The Germans responded with relentless repression focusing on innocent civilian populations. The most brutal of these reprisals occurred on 10 June 1944, when an SS Division, frustrated by its inability to strike a blow against the Allies, murdered around 1,000 men, women, and children in the village of Oradour-sur-Glane (in south-west France). The men were executed while the women and children were burnt alive inside the village church. This razed village can still be visited today. It has been left as it was the day after this atrocity: a painful memorial to the suffering caused by war.

In all occupied countries, the risks were immense. Of the 112,000 French resisters sent to German concentration camps, only 35,000 returned. For those who were captured, torture was routine. As one Czech journalist involved in the clandestine production of newspapers said: 'The way by shooting didn't seriously bother me. It was too common in our country to worry me. But death another way—the slow way—sometimes brought me awake in the night sweating. I had seen some of the results of their handiwork.'[9] Odette Sansom was an SOE agent in the Cannes area of France who paid this price. She was captured, tortured, and eventually sent to the Ravensbrück concentration camp. She describes her experiences:

> I am not courageous. I just make up my own mind about certain things and when they started their treatment of me I'm not going to say that I thought 'This is fun'. I thought well you know there must be a breaking point. Even if in your own mind you don't want to break, but physically you are bound to break up after a certain time I suppose. 'If I can survive the next minute without breaking up, then that's another minute of life.' And if I can feel that way instead of thinking what's going to happen in half an hour's time. Having torn out my toenails they were going to do my fingers, but they were stopped because the commandant came in and said 'Stop!' And then they would burn my back. Of course, there are many other things they can do to me. But if I accept that it will not be my decision, they will kill me. They will kill me physically, but that's all. They won't win anything. What's the point? They will have a dead body, useless to them. But they will not have me.[10]

She survived the ordeal: hundreds of thousands of other resisters did not.

4

Battle of the Atlantic

Battle had begun on land, but, from the moment war was declared, the seas and oceans were the sites of bloody encounters between rival sides. Casualties occurred immediately. In the first week after the declaration of war, thirteen deep-sea merchant ships had already been sunk. 'The only thing that ever really frightened me during the war was the U-Boat peril,' confessed Winston Churchill. He admitted:

> Amid the torrent of violent events one anxiety reigned supreme. Battles might be won or lost, enterprises might succeed or miscarry, territories might be gained or quitted, but dominating all our power to carry on the war, or even to keep ourselves alive, lay in our mastery of the ocean routes and the free approach and entry to our ports.[1]

It was Churchill who coined the phrase 'Battle of the Atlantic' and, like many striking phrases of his that have entered the history books, the Battle of the Atlantic was more a catchphrase than an accurate description. For one thing, the Battle of the Atlantic was not a battle at all nor did it take place only in the Atlantic. It was really a campaign that lasted the entire war, although the most important period was between September 1939 and May 1943. It was global in nature, ranging from the Caribbean to the Pacific Ocean from the Cape of Good Hope to the Barents Sea off the North Cape. Popularly known as a campaign dominated by submarine warfare, the so-called submarines were no such things: they were actually 'submersibles'. Navies had to wait until the 1950s for the invention of true submarines—that is, vessels that operated just as effectively under the water as they did on the surface. However, one thing is indisputable: the Battle of the Atlantic was a struggle against fierce elements of water and wind, as much as a war between machine and man.

'Wolf Packs'

Command of ocean routes was necessary for both Allied and Axis powers. German leaders were well aware that keeping open communications and trade routes was crucial to the British war economy. Without them, the Allies faced defeat by strangulation of their supply lines. The Allies were equally keen to maintain the blockade on Axis nations. Although this chapter focuses on the European Axis nations, the sea routes were also crucial for Japan. As we shall see in a later chapter, the continued domination by America of the sea routes between Japan and Japan's South-East-Asian possessions was devastating for the Japanese economy. In 1942, 40 per cent of the oil from captured oilfields reached Japan: within two years, this was down to a measly 5 per cent. No oil got through in 1945. Deprived of oil, the Japanese war economy was crippled.

Superficially, it seemed as though the Allies had an advantage over the Axis nations in the water, since historically they possessed an indisputable superiority in naval power. However, the small but modern German fleet and submarines were no insignificant threat. Furthermore, the fall of France gave Germany an advantage by providing bases in France and Norway. As a consequence, the German U-boats were initially very successful. Under the command of Grand Admiral Karl Dönitz, they operated as 'wolf packs'. When a convoy was sighted, the submarine would radio the location to land-based headquarters, which would then convey the information to other submarines. Once a number of submarines had convened in a 'pack', they would surface (since this increased their speed substantially), attack the ships with torpedoes, and quickly retreat. The only solution for the Allies was to increase their naval and air escorts in order to prevent the U-boats from getting to their target. They also attempted to destroy as many U-boats as possible along the way, by attacking them with depth charges (that is, 300-pound explosive charges placed inside heavy drums and fired into the sea). Depth charges worked either by directly destroying the U-boat or by forcing it to the surface, where it could be fired upon. In addition to such aggressive ways of dealing with the German threat in the water, the Allies also responded defensively by rationalizing imports and increasing the production of ships.

Although German U-boats remained in action until the very end of the war, the Allies were in the ascendancy by 1943, owing to their superior material and sophisticated sources of intelligence. Figure 3 illustrates the newly found confidence of the Americans and British. Without question,

The Battle of the Atlantic.

3 The Battle of the Atlantic from the Allies' point of view (cartoon by Stephen Roth, Czech artist in exile in London)

intelligence was the key to evading the U-boats. In May 1941, the British captured an 'Enigma' coding machine, enabling them to decrypt German command radio transmissions and reroute their ships accordingly. As a consequence, the Germans faced increasing difficulties locating Allied convoys, and were hard hit by Allied air and surface escorts. The Allies also adopted a policy of forcing the U-boats to go underwater, where, being much slower, they could be attacked more effectively. The use of search radar enabled

Allied vessels to detect U-boats even in poor conditions and at a distance. Allied aeroplanes could then target the U-boats rapidly and with devastating accuracy. In other words, the Allies quickly learnt that aircraft were the best protection for seacraft.

Improved intelligence did not mean that the Battle of the Atlantic was over. Indeed, the ruthlessness of this war increased from late 1942, when the German U-boats began focusing on merchant shipping in American home waters and in the Caribbean, resulting in the loss of nearly 400 ships and severe damage to the Allied war effort. Probably the most notorious of these attacks occurred on 12 September 1942, when German torpedoes sank the *Laconia*. To their great consternation, the German U-boat commanders were surprised to discover that there were 1,800 Italian prisoners of war on board, along with nearly 1,000 other men, women, and children, so they started a rescue operation. Unaware of this rescue operation, an American bomber began attacking the U-boats. Dönitz was livid with fury. He ordered future commanders of U-boats to 'be severe' and forbade them to rescue survivors other than the captains and chief engineers of the enemy ships. Other shipwrecked people were to be rescued only if they were thought to possess valuable information. In the words of his infamous 'Laconia Order': 'Be hard. Remember the enemy has no regard for women and children when he bombs German cities.' At the end of the war, the Nuremberg courts declared that this order was licence to murder. Dönitz was convicted as a major war criminal and imprisoned for ten years in Spandau, the Allied prison in West Berlin.

Effect of the Campaign

Clearly, this was a tough campaign for all concerned, particularly for the ordinary seamen. Naval warfare was very different from battle on land. For seamen, this kind of warfare was a much more detached and impersonal affair. But, even though the enemy was rarely sighted, it was not a wholly bloodless war. Crew reported that they knew that they had made a 'kill' by the 'grim detritus floating on the water' after an attack. As one Commanding Officer bluntly remarked while surveying the seas following one such attack: 'I don't know what it is but the surgeon says it was human.'

Furthermore, the war in the seas was a war of fear as intense as that experienced by people under aerial bombardment. In the North Atlantic, wind, water, and ice were worse enemies than the U-boats, especially during the terrifying winters of 1941 and 1942. The freezing weather also meant that less than half of a crew could even hope to survive if their ship was sunk. The panic of merchant and naval seamen as they scrambled for their lifeboats, and the claustrophobia suffered by U-boat crews awaiting the boom of depth charges, were common experiences. Geoffrey Drummond, a 19 year old serving in the Royal Navy, recalled the frightening environment in which he and his comrades struggled to survive and help others to survive:

> I think probably the things that stand out in my memory more than anything are the cries of people amongst the wreckage after a ship had been torpedoed. The hustle and bustle of climbing into a boat, being lowered, getting it all away, and then, while your own ship may well be some distance away, listening to what might be called 'the quiet of the sea'; but then

the human voices coming into the picture. Where are they? What is the distance? Because in those days quite a number of people didn't have lights on their life-jackets, and quite a number of people that you picked up didn't have life-jackets at all. And so the human cries, the pitiful sort of appearance of the people in the water, getting them into your own boat and then trying to get back to your own ship as quickly as you could to unload that lot and get off for another load.[2]

Thousands of men were simply swallowed up by the waves (see Figure 4, which shows Japanese seamen clinging to the side of their warship as it went down after being bombed).

Yet the outcome of the Battle of the Atlantic was crucial for the war. The cost in terms of material and manpower was high. Around 2,700 Allied merchant ships were sunk, as were 784 U-boats (that is, 80 per cent of the total number of U-boats in operation); 30,000 seamen in the British merchant navy were killed, 20,000 officers and men in Allied warships, and 28,000 German officers and men in U-boats. After the war, the grave danger faced by seamen during the Battle of the Atlantic was often forgotten. For example, in Canada only 4 per cent of members of the army, navy, and air force were killed, compared to 13 per cent of merchant seamen. Yet these merchant seamen in Canada, Britain, and America were not allotted veteran status (and the accompanying benefits) after the war. The stark fact remains that the Battle of the Atlantic has been remembered more for its rare encounters between capital ships than for the much more important day-to-day labour involved in ensuring that trade routes remained open. Thanks to the work of these Allied seamen, oil and armaments continued to be sent to war zones and, more importantly, civilians were fed.

4 Japanese warship under attack by an American bomber, near Amoy, China, 6 April 1945

5

War in China, Burma, and India

L ike the conflict in the oceans of the world, the war in Asia and the Pacific—or the Greater East Asia War, as the Japanese knew it—covered a vast range of operations. Japan did not possess a coherent military-expansionist policy that it pursued without wavering. Instead, there was not one war but several campaigns, opportunistically pursued in Manchuria, China, South-East Asia, and the Pacific Ocean. Allied responses to Japan's expansion can be divided into the Central Pacific campaign, aimed at attacking Japan from the east, the south-west Pacific campaign attacking from the south and east, and the China–Burma–India campaign, attacking from the north and west. This chapter focuses on the last-named campaign.

The war in the Far East was a bitter and vicious war and second only to the war on the Eastern Front in Europe as far as civilian suffering was concerned. It was a war of attrition, guerrilla clashes, and punitive expeditions, in which the Japanese policy of 'Three Alls' ('take all, burn all, kill all') was pursued with ruthless efficiency. The war cost China 2 million military personnel dead and 1.7 million wounded. However, 15 million Chinese civilians also died between

1937 and 1945. Eighty-five per cent of them were peasants, killed mainly by starvation and exposure rather than by direct military action. Deaths were disproportionately high amongst women and female children. Not only did the conflict devastate the Chinese population and economy; it was decisive in a global context as well. After all, of the 2.3 million Japanese troops overseas, 1.2 million were tied down in China. Although often sidelined by Western historians of the Second World War, the war in China was at the heart of the 'world war'.

Japan's Attack on China

Initially, the Japanese were reluctant to go to war against China, but the resurgence of Chinese nationalism and a strengthening Chinese economy were seen as direct threats to Japanese influence in the region. The Japanese took action in 1931, when their troops occupied Manchuria, a border province of China, and turned it into a puppet state. This had wider implications than simply an attack upon Chinese sovereignty. The Japanese takeover of Manchuria directly threatened the interests of the Soviet Union. Would Japan turn its expansionist ambitions northward—to Siberia, for instance? It was strongly in the interest of the USSR to bolster Chinese resistance to the Japanese. Indeed, in the period prior to 1941, China had benefited from more military aid from the USSR than from the western Allies.

Nevertheless, instead of expanding north, the Japanese moved south. By 1937, the conflict had spread to all of eastern China and the war had begun in earnest. Anti-Japanese feeling was exacerbated by the attack by the Japanese on Chinese soldiers and civilians at the Marco Polo Bridge, next to which was a vital railway line, in July 1937. Because of its strategic importance (it was only ten miles west of Beijing), Japanese troops in northern China had been conducting manœuvres in the area. However, on 7 July 1937, after a Japanese night manœuvre during which the Chinese had fired some shells, a Japanese soldier went missing. In retaliation, the Japanese attacked and war commenced. This may rightly be designated the first battle of the Second World War.

By the end of July, Japanese soldiers had not only seized the bridge but taken control of the entire Tientsin–Peking region. The speed with which Japanese troops conquered parts of China was astounding. By 1938, Canton had 'fallen' and, despite notable military victories, including one in the town of Taierzhuang in southern Shantung, where 30,000 Japanese soldiers were killed by Nationalist Chinese troops, the Chinese were at a distinct disadvantage. The Japanese military was vastly superior. As late as 1940, China had only 150 military aircraft compared with the Japanese total of over 1,000. By the end of 1939, the whole of the north-eastern quarter of China was under Japanese occupation. Still, the Chinese did not surrender, forcing Japan to move still further inland, lengthening supply routes and stretching manpower to absolute limits. What followed was a war of attrition.

Chinese Resistance

The Japanese had hoped for a short war, but they under-estimated the tenacity of Chinese resistance. Protest by the Chinese against the Japanese invasion and against the weak response of the Nationalists to the Japanese encroachments began immediately after Manchuria had been occupied. It culminated in 1935 with the 'December Ninth Move-ment', during which tens of thousands of students protested in Tiananmen Square in Peking. Students were crucial to the resistance, moving into rural areas attempting to stimulate revolt. Thus, in 1936, the Peking–Tientsin Student Union produced leaflets written simply in the vernacular, encouraging revolt. These leaflets proclaimed:

> Men, women, children! Listen to what we say: have you seen those things flying overhead every day? Those things are called aeroplanes. Sitting in them are the devils of the Eastern sea, the Japanese devils. They speak in a foreign language, live in the Eastern sea, and fly their aeroplanes over here. Do you know what they are coming to do? . . . They are coming to kill every single man and woman with guns and knives, and to ravish our daughters and wives.[1]

Exhortations like this were produced by resisters from all political persuasions—in particular, the Chinese Communist Party (the CCP) under Mao Zedong and the Kuomintang (the Nationalist Party, or KMT) under Chiang Kai-shek. These two parties had been vigorous enemies, but by 1937 Chiang was forced to give up his fight against the Communists in order to focus attention on defeating the Japanese. A truce was called and a 'united front' formed. This 'united front' was always fragile, but was crucial to the war and, in the end, to the fate of China itself.

Together, the Communists and Nationalists mobilized the Chinese population to resist the extraordinarily powerful Japanese military. Most persuasively, Mao argued that the only way to beat the Japanese was through guerrilla warfare. At some stage, he conceded, the Japanese army would have to be attacked head on, but he warned that premature engagement would be devastating. The guerrillas ensured that much of Japanese strength was employed protecting the railways (a central focus of guerrilla activity) and in 'mopping up' isolated guerrilla units. Figure 5 shows what damage peasant resisters could do. Attrition proved a successful strategy. The Japanese were seriously overstretched by mid-1938.

Nevertheless, in the early years of the war, large numbers of Chinese were collaborating with the Japanese and the puppet governments. As one peasant patiently explained: 'The Japanese soldiers are coming and we only need to complete the harvest and pay taxes in the same way to live in peace as ordinary people.'[2] By 1938, however, Chinese resistance was massive, particularly amongst the Communists. What led to this change?

Historians are split on how best to explain the success of the Chinese Communists in attracting support. Some argue that the skill with which the Chinese Communists led resistance to the Japanese made them popular. Particularly from 1941, the Communist-led guerrillas were scoring numerous victories over the Japanese. Japanese brutality meant that the peasants lauded these Communist victories.

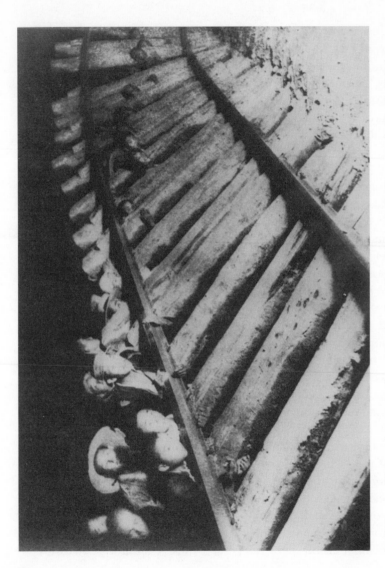

5 Chinese militia and peasants destroying a railway line to impede the Japanese in North China, 1941

There is no question that terror was central to Japanese policy in China. As one Japanese regimental commander boasted: 'Our policy has been to burn every enemy house along the way we advance. You can tell at a glance where our forward units are.'[3] Chinese civilians who were not killed (and in some areas 40 per cent of the population died during the Japanese occupation) were made to perform slave labour or, if young men, forced to serve in the army of one of the puppet governments. Millions of refugees fled to areas still held by the CCP, placing further pressure on resources in Communist-held areas (by 1941 the Communists' Eighth Route Army in the north was in charge of 44 million people).

Other historians argue that it was the CCP's economic programme that brought it support. The peasants and poor suffered an unbearable reduction in their standard of living during the war. Between 1939 and February 1941, for instance, the price of a bushel of rice rose from 2.3 to 32 Chinese dollars. In despair, the poor turned to the Communists for succour. Mao was popular, and able to fuse the rhetoric of communist restructuring with that of nationalism. In other words, the Chinese Communists had a good reputation for attacking the Japanese, but they were also engaged in the struggle for a 'people's resistance' and a peasant revolution. They supported the peasants in their struggle with the landlords. The CCP's policy of reducing rents gave the peasants something they considered well worth fighting for, thus encouraging participation in the resistance. Their slogan, 'there must not be a single idle person, horse, or ox', summed up the Communist campaign, particularly during harvest time.

These two explanations for the popularity of the Communists are not mutually exclusive. In reality, the reason for the growth of Communist resistance in China was most probably a combination of anti-Japanese feeling bolstered by economic promises. As Mao admitted: 'Here [by resisting Japan] there is also a revolutionary movement, because the anti-Japanese struggle is accompanied by a struggle for democracy, better livelihood, and economic construction. Both go together in China. . . . It is also true that along this road the Chinese revolution gains.'[4]

Or, as he reiterated just over a year later, the war was 'being waged to drive out imperialism and transform the old China into a new China'.

Burma, India, and Support from the Western Allies

The Chinese resisters did not have to fight alone. Admittedly, Stalin, Churchill, and Roosevelt had all agreed on a 'Europe-first' policy. Even dissenters from this policy placed victory in the Pacific higher than China's tribulations. Churchill regarded resources sent to China as simply a diversion from India.

Nevertheless, the Chinese were given some help, partly because, in the longer term, China was seen as central to stability in Asia after the war. Only China could hold Japan in check—at least, this was what the Allies (particularly America) believed. In addition, although the other Powers had looked on while Japan invaded parts of China, when the Japanese turned to French Indo-China it became clear that American interests in the Philippines, British interests in

Malaya and Singapore, and Dutch interests in the East Indies were threatened. These campaigns will be discussed in the next chapter.

The Americans were the first of the western Allies to offer military aid. Even prior to the bombing of Pearl Harbor, they provided help through the same lend-lease scheme that had been so important for the British. Then, in July 1941, the USA imposed a financial and oil embargo on Japan, making America Japan's most formidable enemy. After Pearl Harbor, American aid no longer had to be clandestine. Large loans of money were made, and the OSS provided weapons and training to Mao and Ho Chi Minh (leader of the Communist Party of French Indo-China, later known as Vietnam). Henceforth, the resistance forces were heavily dependent upon American aid, especially after 1941, when the Soviet Union was preoccupied with its own fight against Germany.

If China was to be helped, severe logistical problems had to be solved. By 1941, the only way the western Allies could assist China directly was over the mountains through eastern India and north-east Burma. Yet, as we shall see in the next chapter, within hours of bombing Pearl Harbor on 7 December 1941, the Japanese had attacked British Malaya and Thailand, thus posing a direct threat to British Burma. Finally, in 1942, Burma was invaded by the Japanese, who needed to close the Burma Road, which was being used to provide supplies, including precious oil, to Chinese resistance. By early March 1942, the Japanese were in Rangoon, forcing the British, Indian, and Burmese units to retreat northwards into India, while Chinese divisions returned to China. That same month, the Japanese shut off the Burma Road, effectively isolating China from the outside world.

The response of the Allies was twofold: find some way of keeping supplies flowing to the Chinese resisters while continuing to harass the Japanese through small-scale military operations. The first of these problems was ingeniously solved by employing British airbases in India to fly in weapons and other military supplies. These operations came to be termed 'The Hump', because planes flew over the Himalayan mountains. Between December 1942 and VJ Day, the Air Transport Command (one of the main groups transporting supplies) made more than 167,000 trips over 'The Hump', carrying 722,000 tons of supplies.

Indirect military action proved a more difficult problem. The Allies supported Burmese guerrillas (largely composed of Kachins, Karens, Shans, Chins, Lushais, and Palaungs), who were able to wreak havoc behind Japanese lines. The western Allies also did their small share by creating Chindits or 'long-range penetration groups'. The word 'chindits' comes from the Burmese word *chinthe*—that is, the winged lions made of stone that guard Buddhist temples. The British Major-General Orde Wingate, a brilliant guerrilla fighter, established the Chindits. Their main principles were to remain mobile, always to surprise the enemy, and to survive on supplies dropped from aircraft. Wingate taught his men to use the jungle to their own advantage. Their main task was to sever Japanese lines of communication, especially railways. Between mid-February and the end of March 1943, Wingate led his 3,000 Chindits into Burma, where they seriously disrupted Japanese communications. However, in their desperate retreat, many sick and wounded men had to be abandoned. One-third failed to return. In March 1944, Wingate returned with a reinforced group of 9,000 Chindits. When

Wingate died in an aeroplane crash, command was given to the American General 'Vinegar Joe' Stilwell, whose hostility to the Chindits was well known. Stilwell led the Chindits further north, to disastrous effect. The men had been 'in the field' too long and the vast majority died, mainly through disease and malnutrition. As a consequence, the value of the Chindits is a matter of dispute. They have been immortalized, not least because their real importance was not strategic but propagandistic: their actions showed that the Japanese were no longer invincible.

The war to drive the Japanese out of Burma was long and painful. The war of attrition between the two sides resulted in the deaths of 50,000 of the 84,000 Japanese soldiers based there. As one British soldier, Andrew Roy, observed in a letter to his father: 'The war here gets "curiouser and curiouser", to me at any rate. . . . The Jap seems to be getting killed in ever increasing numbers. We seem to be fighting a war to exterminate the Jap wherever he is found rather than a war to secure or win back territory.'[5]

The increasing dehumanization of the Japanese made the killing all the easier. Figure 6 shows one such atrocity. It was not until May 1945 that the British were able to retake Rangoon. Burma was the bloodiest campaign of the Far East for the British, Indian, East African, West African, Chinese, and Japanese soldiers who fought there. The war did not end until after the bombing of Hiroshima in August 1945.

6 Severed head of a Japanese soldier hanging from a tree in Burma. It was presumably put there by American soldiers

Atrocity

Whether the freeing of China from Japanese occupation could have occurred without the dropping of the bombs on Hiroshima and Nagasaki is a controversial question that will be examined much later in this book. What is without dispute, however, is that the Japanese regime in the Far East was brutal. As occurred throughout the Second World War, atrocities flourished alongside feelings of racial superiority. As Figure 7 shows, in Chinese cartoons the Japanese were portrayed as vicious beasts or pirates, tearing apart 'the people'. Even more striking, Japanese propaganda claimed that one Japanese soldier was equivalent to twenty Chinese soldiers. The Chinese were portrayed as cowardly or, according to a popular phrase, the Chinese always 'fled pell-mell like scattering spider babies'.[6] Chinese life was cheap.

The most notorious example of Japanese brutality occurred at Nanking. The diary of one Japanese soldier present at the time described how, 'when we were bored, we had some fun killing Chinese. Buried them alive, or pushed them into a fire, or beat them to death with clubs, or kill them by other cruel means.'[7] In addition to the slaughter, over 20,000 women were raped. Shirô Azuma was a soldier at Nanking who participated in the rapes and murders. He recalled:

> While the women were fucked, they were considered human, but when we killed them, they were just pigs. We felt no shame about it. No guilt. If we had, we couldn't have done it. When we entered a village, the first thing we'd do was steal food, then we'd take the women and rape them, and finally we'd kill all the men, women, and children to make sure they

7 'Eastern Pirate's Speciality' (cartoon by Cai Ruohong). The bodies on the ground are labelled 'people'

couldn't slip away and tell the Chinese troops where we were. Otherwise, we wouldn't have been able to sleep at night.[8]

Partly in response to this lawlessness within the Japanese Imperial Army, the system of 'comfort women' was established. The *ianfu* or *jûgunianfu* were girls and women who had been forcibly recruited or abducted to provide sex for men of the Japanese Imperial Army. In other words, senior personnel in the army argued that the *ianfu* were needed to maintain the soldiers' 'health', both physically and militarily. It was an attempt to stop the epidemic of raping. Approximately 160,000 women were forced to become *ianfu*, of whom 80 per cent were Koreans.

Other atrocities were conducted at the behest of 'science'. The most notorious was conducted in a centre called Unit 731, based near Harbin, in a remote area on the Manchurian Peninsula. Over 3,000 researchers and technicians were employed in Unit 731, under a bacteriologist, Colonel Ishii Shiro. It was here that Japanese scientists conducted a vast programme dedicated to developing biological weapons, including plague, anthrax, cholera, small pox, gangrene, typhus, and typhoid. POWs and Chinese victims were frozen, placed inside pressure chambers to see how long it took before their eyeballs popped from their sockets, or were tied to stakes and bombarded with test weapons. Children as young as 3 years of age were experimented upon. Some prisoners underwent vivisection, without anaesthetic, in order to test the effects of poisonous microbes upon their bodies. A former medical assistant recalled:

The fellow knew that it was over for him, and so he didn't struggle. But when I picked up the scalpel, that's when he began screaming. I cut him open from the chest to the stomach, and he screamed terribly, and his face was all twisted in agony. He made this unimaginable sound, he was screaming so horribly. But then he finally stopped.[9]

It is estimated that over 200,000 Chinese were killed in germ-warfare experiments alone. When Japan surrendered, Unit 731 released thousands of infected experimental animals into the neighbouring area, resulting in a plague epidemic that killed over 20,000 Chinese villagers. The further tragedy was that, after the war, the USA helped cover up the experiments, giving immunity to 3,600 military personnel, doctors, and scientists from Unit 731 in exchange for the data they had collected. As one American researcher said in an attempt to justify this decision: 'such information could not be obtained in our laboratories because of the scruples attached to human experimentation.'[10] Nevertheless, some American (and other) scientists had no scruples about using such data irrespective of its source.

Although China was the location of innumerable atrocities, Burma also saw severe repression. Not even Buddhist monks were safe and their shrines were desecrated. As one Burmese writer was to comment: 'The period of Japanese rule lasted only three years, but to the Burmese people it was more irksome than some sixty years of British rule. . . . The Japanese imposed a reign of terror.'[11] Burma was the scene of one of Japan's harshest labour schemes, the building of the Burma–Siam Railway. This was carried out between November 1942 and October 1943 and traversed 420 kilometres of dense jungle from Bampong in Thailand to Thanbyuzayat in Burma. Around 250,000 labourers from South-East Asia (particularly Chinese, Malay, Burmese, and Javanese) were forced to work on this railway, alongside 60,000 POWs (of whom 700 were American). The railway was completed within six months but at a great cost to life: one-quarter of those working on the railway died. Witnessing the survivors of the railway, one commentator described them thus:

> These survivors of the Burma railway did not look like men—on the other hand, they were not quite animals. They had feet torn by bamboo thorns, working for months without any footwear. Their shins had no spare flesh at all on the calf and looked as if bullets had exploded inside them, bursting the meat outwards and blackening it. These were the ulcers, of which they had dozens ... Heads were shrunken on skulls with large teeth and faintly glowing eyes set in black wells—hair was matted and lifeless. The whole body was draped with a loose-fitting envelope of thin, purple-brown parchment which wrinkled horizontally over the stomach and chest, and vertically on sagging fleshless bottoms.[12]

Such brutality and disregard for life was typical of the entire campaign in Burma and inspired leaders like Wingate to coin phrases such as 'one round—one Jap'.

Civil War

The invasion of China had lasted eight years. This makes it the longest invasion endured by any country during the Second World War. War did not end in 1945, however. As was the case in Europe, the 'world war' was also a civil war. With Japan out of the conflict, China's vicious civil war between Mao's Communists and the Nationalists under Chiang could be pursued with new vigour and concentration. This was inevitable long before the end of the war with Japan. A brutal conflict between the Communist New Fourth Route Army (in the south) and the Kuomintang in January 1941 had signalled their permanent parting. With the end of the war with Japan, the two sides transferred their fight to the 'internal enemy'. It took until 1949 for the Communists to claim victory. In 1949, Mao announced the formation of the Chinese People's Republic from the Gate of Heavenly Peace in Peking.

Mao's victory was due to many factors. The Nationalists paid the price for the ludicrously spiralling inflation, accompanied by corruption, vast inequalities of wealth, and political repression, in areas controlled by them. The Nationalists were seen as hypocritical and corrupt—and everyone had heard the gossip that, while inflation raged, Madame Chiang had rosewood furniture flown in over 'The Hump'. The Nationalists also suffered from poor military leadership. Even Chiang admitted that his generals 'fight muddleheaded battles'.[13] In contrast, Mao effectively deployed his guerrillas and was able to mobilize 'The People'. Guerrilla warfare (known by Chinese Communists as 'sparrow warfare') was crucial, but, even when the People's Liberation Army did engage directly with Nationalist troops, their use of mobile, light-infantry tactics was superior. By mid-1948, the Communist army outnumbered that of the Nationalists and it was a much more effective fighting force. The Communists were also helped by the fact that, once the Soviet Union had taken over Manchuria, they turned north-eastern China over to the Chinese Communists, along with an arsenal of surrendered Japanese weapons. Although this action won them the disapprobation of the other Allies, it was to prove decisive in the civil war. The war in China over, Mao was faced with the daunting task of transforming 'the old China into a new China'. No one envied him: it was to be a long and difficult task.

6

War in South-East Asia and the Pacific

I n the rest of the Asian theatre of war, the Japanese faced opponents from many different countries: Filipinos, Malayans, and Solomon Islanders, as well as Australians, New Zealanders, and British. The key word is 'empire'. For all participants, the campaigns in South-East Asia and the Pacific were imperialistic. America, Britain, the Netherlands, and France had already colonized much of the area, and were not prepared to give it up without a fight. Even America, which had already begun the process of decolonization in the Philippines, was not prepared to see the territory forcibly taken away from it. The Japanese claimed to be fighting a war of liberation, even though the occupation of these countries was central to Japan's expansionist ambitions. Japan, a country smaller than the American state of California, had a population of 74 million to feed and the war in China had proved much more expensive than expected. Japan needed the resources of other East Asian nations to sustain it. Japanese liberationist rhetoric combined with an economic imperative fused neatly into the slogan 'Asia for the Asians within the Greater East Asia Co-Prosperity Sphere', even if (in the words of the Prime Minister of Japan,

General Tojo Hideki) Japan was to be 'the core, the kernel, whereby all states and peoples of Great East Asia will be enabled to find their place in the world'.[1] Mutual prosperity was the goal, but under the guidance of the 'superior' Japanese.

The Japanese Offensive in South-East Asia

Around the same time as Pearl Harbor was attacked, Malaya, the Philippines, Singapore, Thailand, Bangkok, Guam, Wake Island, and Hong Kong also found themselves at war. Map 2 shows the Japanese attacks from December 1941 to March 1942. British Malaya was actually attacked before Pearl Harbor. Its rubber trees and tin mines were just too valuable to bypass and a British Malaya stood in the way of possessing the Dutch East Indies. Malaya could also provide the Japanese with a new naval base and airfields. This campaign was conducted with skill and determination on the Japanese side, and with thoughtlessness and hesitancy on the part of the British. Japanese commanders made effective use of tanks in the jungle, something the British did not think was possible, and they tricked the Allies into believing that they were stronger than they were. In contrast, the Allies suffered from poor leadership, poor training, and low morale. The loss of command at sea was crippling. By 31 January 1942, the British forces (of which over half were Indian) had been forced to retreat to Singapore, where inadequate air strength put the Allies at a great disadvantage. When the Japanese began bombing Singapore, the British mishandled the campaign. Coordination between the three services was

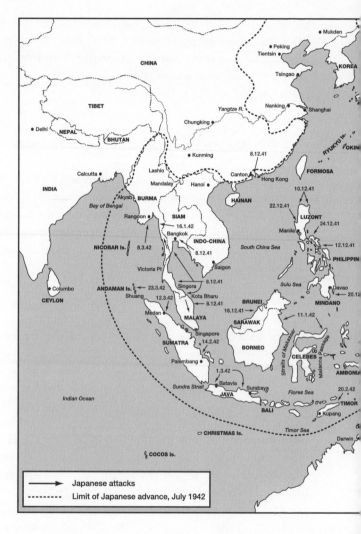

2 The Far East, showing the Japanese attacks between December 19 and March 1942

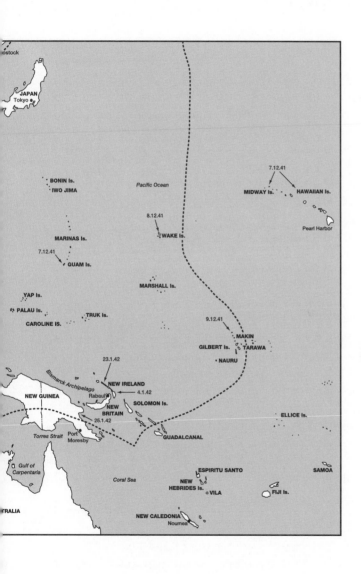

appalling. For instance, the army was instructed to protect the airfields, but the air force did not tell the army where the fields were located. On 15 February 1942, 85,000 Allies surrendered to only 35,000 Japanese. It sent out a key message about imperialism: the white European empire was over; Japanese imperialism would triumph. In the words of Admiral Sir Herbert Richmond, 'Singapore has fallen. It is the greatest disaster that we have suffered since the collapse of France'.[2]

The Japanese changed the name of Singapore to Syonan and then built a shrine (the Syonan Shinto Shrine) near the centre of the battle. In the words of Tsuji Masanobu, Director of Military Operations for the 25th Japanese Army in Singapore, by building the shrine 'in a spirit transcending both gratitude and revenge' the Japanese army 'rendered service to the Gods'.[3] It was to be another three and a half years before the shrine would be blown up and Singapore freed.

The Philippines was also bombed, in an attack that destroyed over half of its military aeroplanes in one blow. Before the end of the month, Japanese troops had landed and the joint American and Filipino army, led by the Commander of the US Forces in the Far East, General Douglas MacArthur, and comprising 15,000 American and 65,000 Filipino soldiers, was on the run. It was poorly equipped (two-thirds of its mortar shells and four-fifths of its grenades were duds) and many of its soldiers were barely trained. They ended up on the Bataan Peninsula. Here, MacArthur commanded his troops inside a large cave, from which he rarely emerged. The rhyme 'the battered Bastards of Bataan, no Papa, no Mama, no Uncle Sam!' was born out of this situation.

MacArthur eventually slipped away to Australia, leaving

8 American POWs with their hands tied behind their backs, just before starting the Death March out of Bataan in April 1942

10,000 Americans and 62,000 Filipinos to surrender. At the time, this was the largest surrender of American troops in the war. As prisoners of war, their ordeal continued. The prisoners were marched by foot 55 miles from Mariveles on the peninsula to the inland town of San Fernando. The march took only seven days but resulted in the deaths of 2,300 Americans and 10,000 Filipinos. After three and a half years in captivity, only one-third of the prisoners were still alive. Figures 8 and 9 respectively show American and Japanese POWs, captured on the Bataan Peninsula during this campaign.

9 Japanese POWs, captured on Bataan, being led blindfolded to the Headquarters for questioning (undated)

However, it was to be 1945 before the Philippines was liberated. Manila was not liberated until February 1945 and only after 100,000 Manilan civilians had been killed, alongside around 1,000 guerrillas and 6,500 American troops. Thus, Japanese occupation lasted until the end of the war and saw the 'blood sacrifice' of young Japanese volunteers reach new heights. Suicidal attackers, known as 'Tokko' in Japan or 'Kamikaze' ('Divine Wind') in Europe, made their first appearance in October 1944 in the battle of the Leyte Gulf (in the Philippines), the largest naval battle ever fought.

The kamikaze attacks were a demonstration of spiritual courage and determination. In the Philippines between October 1944 and January 1945, conventional warfare resulted in the sinking of twelve American warships and the damaging of twenty-five other warships, while kamikaze aircraft destroyed twenty-two ships and damaged a further 110. In other words, although it was honourable to end one's own life in the process of decimating the enemy in a suicidal attack, it was also militarily effective. Nevertheless, the entire archipelago of islands that makes up the Philippines was not freed until Japan surrendered after the dropping of the atomic bombs.

Less than two hours after the bombing at Pearl Harbor, the Japanese invaded and conquered Thailand. They were keen to make use of Thailand's rice surpluses. Here, the outcome was different. On 21 December, the Thais signed a 'Treaty of Alliance' with Japan and, within a month, declared war on Britain and America. Because of this Treaty, the Thais were not treated as harshly as the Chinese or, as we shall see later, the Filipinos. Nevertheless, the Japanese did place a huge burden on the economy, especially in May 1945, when they demanded several million baht from Thai funds.

Slightly later than the other conquests, on 11 January 1942, the Japanese invaded the Dutch East Indies (which included Sumatra, Java, Bali, the Celebes, and parts of Borneo, West New Guinea, and East Timor). The Netherlands had been occupied eighteen months earlier, so could not help the Dutch East Indies. Australia, America, and Britain came to their aid, but within two months the Japanese had triumphed once more. In particular, the Allies' navies suffered an inglorious defeat at the Battle of the Java Sea on 27 February 1942. This was the first fleet action of the Pacific War, and a bad omen. A few thousand Dutch troops managed to escape to Australia, but over 60,000 soldiers and 100,000 Dutch civilians were captured. A large proportion never survived the end of the war. As happened everywhere, civilians suffered extensively. During the Japanese occupation, around 3.7 million Indonesians died at the end of a bayonet, through overwork as slave labourers, or as a result of malnutrition and disease.

Collaboration and Resistance

For many of the South-East Asian countries, Japanese military occupation was simply another form of colonial rule. In the early days of the occupation, the Japanese attempted to win the indigenous peoples over. The ideal of the Greater East Asia Co-Prosperity Scheme involving economic and political cooperation was emphasized and cultural re-education was carried out energetically through radio, drama, exhibitions, the press, music, and film. In a bid for support against the western Allies, in November 1943 Japan hosted the Great East Asia Conference, with representatives from the Philippines, Burma, and Siam, at which Japan's 'lofty aims in the moral war she is waging against the Anglo-Americans' were proclaimed. General Tojo poured scorn on the hypocrisy of the western imperial nations and promised the 'autonomy and independence' of nations belonging to the 'Greater East Asia' as well as spiritual resurgence. As Jimbo Kotaro, Japanese poet and a leading member of the Propaganda Unit in Malaya, described it: 'It is a heaven sent mission for the *Yamato* race to guide the indigenous population.'[4]

Initially at least, the Japanese were welcomed as fellow Asians by many of the peoples they conquered. As the Burmese Prime Minister, Ba Maw, said, his countrymen and women felt 'a new conviction that their old country would be great again and Buddhism recover its old glory'.[5] Similarly, one Filipino recalled that the occupiers

> intended to preserve some of our freedoms, including those of religious worship, recreation, and higher education. It seemed they desired friendship with the nation. Soon we were finding ourselves vassals to their ideology ... of moral rejuvenation, dedication to the orientation of their leadership in Asia, indoctrinating us with the ideals of a 'co-prosperity sphere' and 'Asia for the Asians'.[6]

Soetan Sjahrir, nationalist leader in Indonesia, complained about widespread frustration at being treated like inferiors by the Dutch, claiming that his pro-Japanese stance was 'a projection of a frustrated desire for freedom'.[7]

As part of this process, the Japanese trained and armed thousands of South-East Asians to support them as auxiliary troops or as armies fighting for independence from the western colonizers. Of the latter groups, the Indian National Army (INA) was one of the most notable. Captain Mohan Singh, first leader of the Indian National Army in Malaya, argued that there was a huge gap between Japan's promise of Asian liberty and the fact that 'the British had not given even an empty promise to grant us complete freedom after the war'.[8] For him, British slogans of 'Fight for the liberty of mankind' sounded 'quite hollow and meaningless'. The

INA was recruited from the 45,000 Indian troops who became prisoners of the Japanese after the fall of Singapore. About half of these prisoners volunteered to serve in this army, but its strength was greatly enhanced when the charismatic Subhas Chandra Bose took charge, winning over the Indian community in Malaya. Unusually, the INA included an all-female combat unit, the Rani of the Jhansi regiment, composed of about 1,000 Indian, Thai, and Burmese women. Many of these women were to become important in the new Indian nation from 1947. As one historian put it: 'Japan was their enemy's enemy.'[9] Such collaborationist armies gained a considerable degree of support both from the local populations but also from the Japanese, who believed that encouraging Asian aspirations for independence furthered the great cause of 'Asia for Asians'. The Japanese officers who liaised with these local nationalists were often idealistic, even to the extent of seeing themselves as heirs to Lawrence of Arabia, the dashing British officer who had aided the Arabian Bedouins in their fight against the Turks during the First World War.

However, in all occupied countries in South-East Asia, the appeal to pan-Asian sentiments began to lessen, particularly after 1942. On the one hand, this was when the tide began to turn against Japan militarily: maintaining firm ties with Japan was becoming risky. Not only had the Japanese failed to deliver on the economic promises; they no longer seemed quite so omnipotent. On the other hand, the suffering of indigenous peoples in the Japanese-occupied territories was becoming unbearable. Many of the worse atrocities were carried out by the Japanese military police, the Kempeitai, of whom there were around 36,000 in Manchuria, Korea,

10 A survivor of Kalagon Village, north of Moulmein in Burma, picking out members of the Kempeitai at an identity parade at Moulmein Jail

South-East Asia, and the Pacific by the end of the war. After the war many were identified and punished. The survivor of Kalagon Village shown in Figure 10 was one of only five survivors of a massacre of 637 villagers during July 1945.

Terror was commonplace in every occupied country. Prisoners of the Japanese occupiers bore a large share of suffering. One in four Allied prisoners captured by the Japanese died, in contrast with one in twenty western Allied prisoners held by the Germans. Brutality, starvation, and hard work in coal mines, steel mills, docks, roads and railways, airfields, and factories took its toll. For most Japanese soldiers, the mere fact that a person had surrendered was so dishonourable that it justified abuse. Japanese leaders emphasized the idea of *gyokusai*, or fighting to the last man. It was dishonourable even to consider surrender, even when staring defeat in the face. Much better, indeed, to commit suicide or help your comrades to do the same. To surrender meant forfeiting the right to respect. The fact that the Allies had been acting in a racially superior manner was further provocation.

Civilians also suffered. In Malaya and Singapore there was massive repression by the Japanese, especially of the Chinese community, thousands of whom were systematically massacred. The Japanese in the Dutch East Indies set out to destroy all remnants of Dutch culture, including the language. Radios were forbidden and schoolchildren were taught to bow and sing the *kimiga yo*, the Japanese national anthem. Greta Kwik was a 16-year-old Dutch girl from Java. Fifty years after the war she told her story of the occupation:

> I may still have the piece of paper on which Queen Wilhelmina of the Netherlands wrote that she was sorry about what happened. I never looked for it because everything still hurts. When we received it, much, much later, it finally dawned on me that my father was dead. I remember crying and banging my head against a wall in utter sorrow. I do not want to know how my father died. Was he standing, blindfolded, and shot? Did he have to kneel, hands bound behind his back, and have his head chopped off, to topple in a grave of his own digging? ... I have waited for my father all my life ... For most of the past 50 years, I have shed a tear every January 29, his execution date.[10]

In the Philippines, disgust with the occupation grew particularly strongly from 1943 onwards. In October of that year the Japanese had granted the Philippines independence, but it was an independence *vals wals* (of no value), since the Japanese remained in occupation. Civilians as well as prisoners of war were caught up in atrocities. As elsewhere, rape was a central act of war, as was torture (most notoriously, at Fort Santiago). Ralph Levenberg of Clinton, Iowa, was a 20-year-old truck driver when he was captured on the Bataan Peninsula and marched inland to the prison camp. His story is harrowing. He described what happened to a young Filipino woman who was giving birth:

> A Japanese sergeant was walking around, hitting men with the butt of his rifle. He was drunk and just making sure that everybody knew he was 'the big man'. This sergeant just pushed the women all away. He found a piece of wire and tied the gal's legs together at her thighs. She was screaming at the top of her voice, and then he takes his bayonet out and hits her right between the breasts and cuts her open in front of everybody. Now, this American and I were not about to stand around and see what the Japs might do to us, so we slowly made our way back to the line of march . . . That was the first atrocious crime that we saw, other than the beheading of our own people. That happened all along the march, not just with our group. You could see bodies strewn all over. Nothing in my life had prepared me for this kind of brutality. You had to shut it off and just get through one day at a time. You had to, because . . . [*sic*] it was almost like a dream, like you were going to wake up one of these days and none of this happened.[11]

This was only one instance of thousands that took place during the occupation of the Philippines. Nevertheless, the situation became worse after the Allies had landed. While Japanese troops were retreating northwards, they indulged in an orgy of atrocity. Women (even nuns) were raped, babies were tossed in the air and bayoneted, and there were mass executions by decapitation. The 'razing of Manila', as it was to be known, was one of the great war crimes of the century.

The discontent stimulated by the reign of terror was easily harnessed by resistance movements that grew up in many areas of South-East Asia. Resisters engaged in subversion, sabotage, espionage, and attacking Japanese troops. These movements were diverse, both politically and ethnically. For instance, the Chinese-dominated Malayan People's Anti-Japanese Army was a revolutionary, Communist resistance movement, while the Chinese Nationalist Party was a con-servative, nationalist resistance group in Malaya. Some accepted help from the Allies, especially from the SOE (known by the code name of Force 136 in Thailand) and the OSS. Others refused aid from the former western colonizers. By 1945, even the Japanese-trained units in Burma and Java were in revolt. In other words, by the end of the war, 'independence armies' were acting to free their countries from the yoke of their oppressors, whether western or Asian.

The Pacific War: 'Island Hopping'

While the Japanese were occupying South-East Asia, other Japanese troops continued moving southwards into the Pacific. From this point on, the story becomes more con-fusing. The campaigns in the Pacific involved people from hundreds of big and small nations scattered throughout the ocean. Without question, however, the Americans were militarily pre-eminent. Despite the 'Europe First' policy, the US navy allocated two-thirds of its strength to the Pacific theatre. The Americans were in charge of directing the war in the Pacific and they dominated the naval war, but a substantial proportion of the land troops and aircrew were Australian. Indeed, in October 1943, there were nearly 500,000 Australian land troops in the Pacific compared with less than 200,000 American land troops. The reason for the significant participation of the Australians is obvious: they were under direct threat. In March 1942, the Australian Prime Minister, John Curtin, sent out a strong message to America, saying:

> This is a warning. Australia is the last Allied bastion between the west coast of America and Japan. If she succumbs, the entire American Continent will be wide open to invasion. Some people think that the Japanese will bypass Australia and that they will be intercepted and destroyed in the Indies. But I tell you that saving Australia will be the same as saving the western side of the United States. However that may be, Australia will, if invaded, fight to the last man and will apply the scorched earth policy.[12]

In the Pacific campaign, the Japanese were determined to conquer the countries south (for instance, New Guinea and the Solomon Islands and, possibly, Australia) and west (for instance, Hawaii) of the Japanese homeland. Along the way, small nations were to be simply squashed. In contrast, the Allies were desperate to push the Japanese back north. Many expectations had to be jettisoned along the way. For instance, the Americans had planned for 'blue-water' combat (that is, high seas and big guns), but they had slowly to adapt themselves to 'brown water' (riverine and estuarine) and 'white water' (coastal) battle. Indeed, they often found themselves facing the enemy on the shore. Flexibility was central, as was the role of intelligence. Without the secret weapons of 'Ultra' and 'Magic' (breaking German and Japanese codes), the war in the Pacific would have been even more protracted. By early 1944, America was deciphering 20,000 Japanese army messages each month. Finally, it was a war that taught the Allies the importance of 'island hopping'—that is, avoiding strongly held Japanese islands and simply isolating them. It was a policy of 'hit 'em where they ain't'.

It is impossible to do justice to the innumerable campaigns of the war in the Pacific. Instead, this book will just mention four of the most important areas of battle—New Guinea, the Solomon Islands, the Mariana Islands, and Iwo Jima. Although not fully representative, these campaigns represent the complexity of battle in the Pacific.

New Guinea (an island three times the size of Great Britain) is just north of Australia. By early 1942, the Japanese had already captured Rabaul, where they dug tunnels and caves in which their troops could shelter from Allied bombing. This important fortress was the key to Japanese domination of the south and south-west Pacific and was to be the port from which they planned to invade Port Moresby. For the Allies, preventing the Japanese from setting up a secure base in Port Moresby, the capital of New Guinea, was crucial, if Australia was to remain safe from Japanese aircraft. Thus, a bitter struggle began between the Japanese, Australians, and Americans in difficult terrain, thick jungle, and stifling weather. The New Guineans were caught in between. Tens of thousands of villagers were killed, often through indiscriminate bombing. Both the Allies and Axis enlisted their labour (sometimes forcibly) from the indigenous population. The euphemistic phrase 'living off the land' actually meant raiding the crops and animals of the islanders. When this was insufficient, some Japanese soldiers turned to cannibalism. Thus, the starving Japanese 18th Army ate Arapesh people in 1945. One Papua New Guinea man, Arthur Duna, described what happened when the Japanese first landed near their village:

> All the clans . . . who were once brave, courageous, and strong seemed to become like babies in their first day out of their mother's womb. The landing of the Japanese, gun noises, and the actual sight of the ships seemed to have removed the bones of the people. They could not run and even if they did try to run, they could not. It was a unique disaster beyond anybody's memory.[13]

For servicemen on both sides, the iconic horror of this campaign was the Kokoda Trail, leading across the mountains to Port Moresby. On this 1,610-kilometre mountain trail, thousands perished. Ogawa Masatsugu fought for the Japanese in New Guinea from January 1943 until the end of the war. Although he recalled the great brutality of the campaign, in which many soldiers committed suicide, the months of marching in an unrelenting climate remained his most vivid memory. In his words:

> It rained for more than half a year straight. Our guns rusted. Iron just rotted away. Wounds wouldn't heal. Marching in the rain was horrible. Drops fell from my cap into my mouth mixing with my sweat. You slipped and fell, got up, went sprawling, stood up, like an army of marching mud dolls. It

went on without end, just trudging through the muddy water, following the legs of someone in front of you . . . All battle-fields are wretched places. New Guinea was ghastly. There was a saying during the war: 'Burma is hell; from New Guinea no one returns alive.'[14]

In the end, as with all the campaigns in the Pacific, naval warfare was crucial. The Battle of the Coral Sea on 4–8 May 1942 prevented the Japanese from seizing Port Moresby. This was the first naval battle fought solely with aircraft and without the ships actually seeing each other. Although the Americans lost a carrier, they prevented the Japanese from taking New Guinea. The Americans had the advantage, in that, through the use of 'Ultra', they could read Japanese codes, enabling them to locate, bypass, and outflank the enemy. They also learnt the lesson that the aircraft carrier rather than the battleship was to be crucial to victory in naval warfare.

For the Japanese, the Battle of Midway followed this humiliating defeat in the Coral Sea. Midway was important for the Japanese because it would provide a base from which they could threaten Hawaii. Again, the Battle of Midway in early June 1942 was rendered a victory for America because 'Ultra' intelligence enabled them to prepare for the invasion of Midway Island. Four Japanese carriers were sunk com-pared with only one American carrier. Midway was the first decisive defeat of the Japanese in the Pacific War. After Mid-way, the Japanese were on the defensive and their expansive drive stopped. From this time onwards, the Japanese were forced to evacuate one island after another.

One series of islands that the Japanese were keen to retain was the Solomon Islands (which included Bougainville,

Choiseul, New Georgia, and Guadalcanal). For the Japanese, this chain of islands was important, because it would enable them to sever the connection between Australia, New Zealand, and the USA. On the other side, these same islands could provide the Allies with a ladder upwards to enemy islands in the Carolines. Everyone recognized their value as air and naval bases.

On 7 August 1942, 10,000 American troops landed on Guadalcanal and surrounding islands and the bloody battle commenced, with the Americans being helped by the Solomon Island Defence Force (popularly known as the South Sea Scouts). It was a harsh battle, fuelled by racist beliefs on all sides. Some of the men who fought had had experience fighting the Germans, and the comparison they made between these two Axis troops was to the detriment of the Japanese. In the words of one Marine in Guadalcanal, the Germans

> are human beings, like us. Fighting against them must be like an athletic performance—matching your skill against someone you know is good. Germans are misled, but at least they react like men. But the Japanese are like animals. Against them you have to learn a whole new set of physical reactions. You have to get used to their animal stubbornness and tenacity. They take to the jungle as if they had been bred there, and like some beasts you never see them until they are dead.[15]

The Guadalcanal campaign ended in February 1943. It was the first successful American land battle in the Pacific and, once again, the outcome had been greatly influence by 'Ultra' intelligence and American air and sea superiority. Nevertheless, victory was achieved only by extreme means. Of the 60,000 Americans who fought, 1,600 were killed. In contrast, of the 36,000 Japanese who fought, 15,000 were missing or dead, 10,000 died of sickness, and 1,000 were captured. None of these figures includes those who were killed at sea. After Guadalcanal, the Japanese adopted a policy of 'Campaign First'—that is, all their energy had to be devoted to defending areas already under Japanese occupation.

The New Georgia group of islands was liberated next, followed by Bougainville and New Britain. In all cases, guerrilla groups were important. Allied victory was never total, however. Despite the fact that Allied troops were in control of the Solomon Islands by 1943, the Japanese army, navy, and air force did not surrender and the fighting really only ended with the conclusion of the war in 1945.

Meanwhile, the Allies reached the Mariana Islands, which included Saipan, Tinian, Rota, and Guam. The capture of these islands was crucial: it would make the Japanese homeland vulnerable to bombers. Bitter fighting took place, particularly on Tinian and Saipan, which had large Japanese garrisons. The Americans invaded Saipan in June 1944. On this island, as with so many others during the war in the Pacific, if evacuation could not take place, the Japanese troops and civilians chose to commit suicide—most famously in Saipan, where, on 7 July 1944, 25,000 Japanese civilians committed suicide rather than be taken prisoner. The sight of civilian women leaping from cliffs was an unforgettable memory for the veterans of this campaign. Nevertheless, 14,700 Japanese colonists and Chamorros surrendered.

Finally, the war moved to Iwo Jima. This was a little volcanic island less than 8 square miles in size but crucial to the Japanese because, being 660 miles south of Tokyo, it provided air-raid warnings for the Japanese mainland. It was heavily garrisoned with 21,000 troops. Japanese defence was based on a series of tunnels, caves, and gun emplacements. On 19 February 1945, three divisions of American Marines landed. The bloodiness of the campaign can be judged by the fact that 30,000 Americans, 110,000 Japanese, and 150,000 Okinawans were killed. Despite the contrast in the numbers killed of each nationality, for the Americans, the cost in American lives brought the use of the atomic bomb one step closer. It was the last battle between American and Japanese troops in the war.

It was not only human lives that were lost. National treasures were also destroyed. Thus, Okinawa's Shuri castle—a beautiful sixteenth-century monument, artistic and spiritual treasure, and national symbol—was destroyed by the 14-inch guns fired from the battleship *Mississippi*. The island was devastated by a 'typhoon of steel'. Seizen Nakasone, an Okinawan schoolteacher, wrote:

> Among those who narrowly survived the battle, there is a common feeling inexplicable to others ... A certain feeling toward life that is shared only by those who have leaned over and peered into the abyss called death. ... I shouted in my heart: let no trees grow, no grass sprout on that hill [the site of Shuri castle] until all the peoples of the world have seen this ruin wrought by the Battle of Okinawa.[16]

The Effect of the Conflict

The war in the Pacific was protracted and indecisive. While the Japanese had gained their principal objectives within five months, it took the Allies four years to recover them. Each campaign was vicious, particularly for the local residents of the islands. Too often, the various countries occupied during the war in the Pacific are viewed as simply a backdrop and their inhabitants as invisible or, at the very most, mere pawns in a titanic struggle between the major colonial powers, whether Asian or western. Such an approach encourages the dehumanization that leads to atrocities in the first place.

In explaining the viciousness of the war in the Pacific, the virulent racism of all the participating countries is crucial. Japanese commanders believed that they were fighting an imperialistic, materialistic, and degenerate enemy whose chief aim was to pervert the purity of the *Yamato* race. As we saw in the campaigns in South-East Asia, their treatment of prisoners of war and civilians on the islands was exceptionally cruel.

On the other side, the Allies regarded the Japanese as an inferior, brutish population. Thus, Admiral William F. Halsey congratulated the troops who seized the island of Peleliu in October 1944 with the words: 'The sincere admiration of the entire Third Fleet is yours for the hill blasting, cave smashing extermination of 11,000 slant-eyed gophers. It has been a tough job extremely well done.'[17]

Allied troops in the Pacific styled themselves as 'rodent exterminators'. Such attitudes facilitated atrocities. For instance, American troops raped civilian women (particularly on Okinawa), took souvenirs from corpses, and killed prisoners of war. As one Marine put it: 'Nobody wanted to take prisoners to begin with—nobody who had had a buddy killed, which was almost everybody. And nobody wanted to go somewhere to do it—leave his living buddies to walk the prisoners back behind the lines. Why take the risk?

When they first started surrendering, we shot as many as we took.' Allied soldiers had to be bribed with promises of ice cream and time behind the lines before they could be persuaded to take more prisoners. Racist views also meant that the Allies underestimated the ability of the Japanese to wage total war. Indeed, Allied feelings of racial superiority and ignorance of Japanese military culture almost lost them the war.

The war was particularly harsh for the islanders. Neither Japanese nor Allied troops showed the islanders the same degree of respect as they did the South-East Asians. They did not regard the islanders as possessing a culture worth preserving. For Japanese troops, occupation of the islands was more strategic than economic (the islands were important as bases and as a protective shield rather than for precious resources that the Japanese wanted to exploit), so they had little interest in making concessions to the local populace.

As a result, the war was devastating for island culture. Suddenly these islanders were confronted with the military might of Japan, America, Australia, and Britain and forced to accommodate themselves to alien cultures. On many islands, the people were recruited by different sides and thus ended up killing each other. The psychological impact of such terrorization upon local communities can scarcely be imagined. The suffering was greatest on islands such as Bougainville and New Guinea, where there was extensive jungle warfare, and on islands such as Enewetak (one of the Marshall Islands), where there were amphibious assaults. On these islands, the civilian populations were unable to flee. One man from an island just south of Enewetak described how

All of us were in holes. Anything not in the holes disappeared. But even in the holes there was damage ... In the holes it was awful. We were hungry and thirsty, but no one could go out. If you travelled outside you would disappear. The hole was also bad because we had to pee and shit inside, even desecrate the face of close kin. Then in their coming the [American] warriors were not straight in their working. They came to the shelter of ours, guns ready, and looked toward us inside. So great was our fear that we were all in a corner, like kittens. And then they yelled and threw in a hand grenade ... When it burst, the whole shelter was torn apart ... Earth fragments struck us, but the others in the other half, they died.[18]

The islands were turned into scrapyards, littered with rusting military equipment. In the long term, the economic impact was devastating as well. Their economies were often totally destroyed. New relations of exchange and production were forced upon them. Villages suspected of collaborating with the enemy—whichever it might be—were razed. Entire communities were displaced—sometimes deliberately, as in the Green Islands, where the Americans shipped the entire population to Guadalcanal. Tens of thousands were killed.

In the end the superior Allied resources were decisive in both South-East Asia and the Pacific. Most importantly, American ships that were destroyed were replaced quickly. The Allies possessed radar (which the Imperial Japanese Navy lacked), superb intelligence through 'Magic' and 'Ultra', and 40-millimetre guns. Crucially, the Allies' victory was strengthened by the ability of their submarines to destroy Japanese shipping. The Japanese needed 6 million tons of merchant shipping to maintain links with their empire, yet, within the first two years of the conflict, 5 million tons had been destroyed. Japanese industry was incapable of making up for such heavy losses. Furthermore, while Allied troops were well supplied and supported, Japanese troops were scattered amongst a large number of small islands without reliable supplies. Japanese strategy in the Pacific was excessively focused on the idea of defensive warfare, fought from a line of secure island bases. In other words, the Japanese fought according to the naval equivalent of the Maginot Line. This discounted the ability of the Allied air force and navy to isolate and attack the islands, one by one. Mobility was the key—as the Allies understood early on. Carriers and, later, bombers would win this war, not battleships. With painstaking slowness, the Japanese were pushed back north to their homeland, but the war in South-East Asia and the Pacific did not end because of thousands of isolated armageddons: the participants (both military and civilian) had to await a much more terrifying vision—the mushroom cloud of the atomic bomb.

7

Italy, the Balkans, and the Desert

War in Italy, the Balkans, Libya, Egypt, and North Africa was conducted in a confusion of landscapes, from lush mountainous terrain to the vast expanse of desert. Although there were no clashes as impressive as those occurring on the Eastern Front, fascist domination of southern Europe and access to valuable oilfields meant that the stakes were high. These campaigns are also a clear illustration of a central trait of the entire war: in many of its components, it was a civil war. In Italy, Yugoslavia, and Greece, the war was fuelled by internal dissension as well as by international intervention. Ethnic groups, religious affiliations, and social classes fought each other with a fury that was equal to that dedicated to the fascist and anti-fascist struggle. Finally, unlike campaigns elsewhere in Europe, the war in the Balkans and the desert was sparked off by one of Hitler's partners—Italy. It was not inevitable that Mussolini and the Italians would side with fascist Germany. Indeed, on 16 May 1940, Churchill sent a heart-rending plea to Benito Mussolini (the Italian dictator), reminding him of their meetings in Rome. He urged:

Is it too late to stop a river of blood from flowing between the British and the Italian peoples? . . . Down the ages above all other calls comes the cry that the joint heirs of Latin and Christian civilization must not be ranged against one another in mortal strife. Hearken to it, I beseech you in all honour and respect before the dread signal is given.[1]

Passionate words, but they fell on deaf ears.

The Italian Saga in Greece

Although he dithered for a long time, Mussolini eventually signed the Pact of Steel on 22 May 1939, thus fusing the fates of Germany and Italy. Despite the promises in the Pact, Mussolini wished to delay going to war for as long as possible. Furthermore, he was not prepared to be subordinate to Hitler, conceiving his conflict as a 'parallel war'. In Mussolini's words: 'Not for Germany, not with Germany, but by Germany's side'—this was a war fought primarily for Italian rather than German interests. Indeed, Mussolini did not declare war on Britain until 10 June 1940, having been spurred on by the ease with which Hitler's armies had conquered France.

By this stage, however, Mussolini had already made a serious error of judgement. Instead of focusing on only one campaign at a time, he launched two simultaneously, against neutral Greece and against the British in Egypt. On 7 April 1939, Italy had invaded Albania and, from this country, began launching attacks on Greece after war between Italy and Greece had been declared on 28 October 1940. This was an ill-conceived conflict. The Italians attacked at a time when overcast skies hindered full employment of their aircraft. The Italian army was poorly led and even lacked adequate maps of Greece. The indiscreet gossip of the Italian Foreign Minister meant that the Greeks had forewarning of the invasion. Exacerbating the situation, the Italian troops were inadequately prepared for the climate. When the Army General Staff, Marshal Pietro Badoglio, explained to Mussolini, 'Do you not know that we have not enough shirts for our soldiers—I do not say uniforms, but shirts,' the Duce allegedly retorted: 'I know, but I need only a few thousand dead, so that I shall be able to sit at the peace table with the victor.'

Mussolini may have expected a quick and easy victory, but he was to be disappointed. Greek resistance was powerful and effective (see Figure 11). In less than a month, the invaders had been driven from Greek soil, making Greece the first country in Europe to win a victory against an Axis power. It was a victory that was celebrated in all the Allied countries. For the Italians, there was only embarrassment. The centre of Rome had sported a giant map of Greece in order to display the military's triumphs to all Italian citizens. It was quietly removed.

The conflict continued into Albania, where once again the Greeks (with the support of some RAF squadrons) proved themselves vastly superior to the Italians in mountain warfare. Intelligence gained from the 'Enigma' machine enabled two British cruisers and five destroyers to sink three Italian cruisers and two destroyers on 16 March 1941, effectively weakening the Italian navy and giving rise to the quip 'Greek sailors like ouzo, British sailors prefer whisky, but the Italians stick to port'.

11 'The Heroines of 1940', a Greek poster in tribute to the Greek resistance to the Italian invasion of 1940

Germany could not allow this series of defeats to go unchallenged. Hitler had not been told about the invasion of Greece before it happened, but he could not risk damaging the reputation of Axis powers in the eyes of neutral states like Turkey, Yugoslavia, Bulgaria, and Spain, which he hoped to win over to his side. German commanders were also supremely aware that a free Greece threatened more than just a fascist Italy and the reputation of the Axis. British airbases on Greek soil placed at risk German access to the Romanian oilfields, crucial for the planned offensive against the USSR. Consequently, on 6 April 1941, Germany committed two divisions to invading both Yugoslavia and Greece.

The Invasion of Yugoslavia

In order to attack Greece via Bulgaria, Hitler needed to bring Yugoslavia 'on board'. When Prince Paul of Yugoslavia eventually signed the Tripartite Pact with Germany in March, Serbian nationalists rose in protest, overthrowing the government and setting off major public protests against the Pact. Hitler was furious and, on 6 April 1941, in an attack called 'Operation Punishment', bombed Belgrade and other towns. At the same time, German troops, followed by Italians and Hungarians, invaded Yugoslavia. By mid-April, the King had fled and Belgrade was on its knees. The Yugoslav air force and navy were rapidly destroyed or captured and in less than a fortnight Yugoslavia was divided between Germany, Italy, Hungary, and Bulgaria.

As part of the dismemberment of Yugoslavia by the Axis,

an 'Independent State of Croatia' was set up. Under Ante Pavelić, the collaborationist Croatian Ustaše movement established a particularly brutal fascist police state. The Ustaše enthusiastically killed Jews, Serbs, and Gypsies—often by hacking them to death with primitive implements. As a prominent Croatian and Ustaše intellectual, A. Seitz, predicted on 24 June 1941: 'The bell tolls. The last hour of those foreign elements, the Serb and the Jew, has arrived. They shall vanish from Croatia.' A Ustaše priest, Revd Dijonizije Jurichev, agreed: 'In this country, nobody can live except Croatians. We know very well how to deal with those that oppose conversion [to Roman Catholicism]. I personally have put an end to whole provinces, killing everyone—chicks and men alike. It gives me no remorse to kill a small child when he stands in the path of the Ustaše.'[2] According to one estimate, such believers killed around 40,000 Gypsies and 400,000 Serbs in Croatia and Bosnia.

The Ustaše was an extreme example, even amongst Croatian Catholics. Elsewhere in the divided Yugoslavia, repression was also characteristic, and led to the establishment of resistance movements. Resistance in Yugoslavia was extremely complicated. Alongside the struggle against German, Italian, and Croatian fascism, civil war was raging between the Communist partisans and the resistance movement of the Chetniks. The Chetniks were royalist Serbs, organized loosely under the leadership of Colonel Dragoljub (Draža) Mihailović, the Minister of the Army in the exiled government. Their exclusive brand of Serbian nationalism made them unwilling to draw non-Serbs into alliance. Croats, Slovenes, and other minorities would have nothing to do with them. The Chetniks were also incapable of coordinating broad schemes of mobilization, as they were organized on a territorial basis and lacked a strong ideological goal. Mihailović's movement was primarily a military one, aimed at returning the King to Yugoslavia. The members were only loosely tied together by anti-Communist sentiments and a vague loyalty to King Peter.

In contrast, the Communist partisans were led by the part-Croatian Josip Broz (more famously known as Tito), the leader of the Communist Party of Yugoslavia (the KPT). In 1941, the KPT had 8,000 members. But, unlike the Chetniks, the partisans were able to win support amongst the Muslims and Catholic Croats, in addition to Orthodox Serbs. As a consequence, the partisans were able to convert themselves into a People's Liberation Army, with Tito as the Supreme Commander. By 1943, Tito could boast 20,000 fighters, women as well as men. Their struggle was as much against domestic reactionaries, including the Chetniks and the government-in-exile, as fascist occupation. Ignoring pleas by the Comintern to cooperate with the other anti-fascists, Tito set out to achieve a Communist revolution at the same time as ending fascism.

For the Germans, both the Communist partisans and the Chetniks had to be destroyed. They insisted upon loyalty to the German-sponsored regime of General Nedić in Serbia and the Ustaše regime in Croatia. On the ground, however, local Italian and German commanders had a more subtle appreciation of the ideological differences between the two groups and often supported the Chetniks against the partisans. The Italians were particularly likely to take this view, fearing that the Ustaše regime was excessively pro-German. To Hitler's great consternation, some Italians even began collaborating with the Chetniks against the Ustaše regime. If there was an Allied invasion of the Balkans, such disloyalty could be disastrous for the Germans, since half of Germany's oil came from the Balkans, as did most of the war materials for Rommel's armies in Africa.

The conflict between all these groups intensified from 1943. In an attempt to destroy Mihailović and the Chetniks completely, Tito negotiated with the Germans, promising to stop harassing German troops if they would allow the partisans to return home. This enabled the partisans to launch an all-out attack against the Hercegovinian, Bosnian, and Montenegrin Chetniks, with much success. But the truce was short-lived. Many Communist partisans were subsequently killed by the Germans and the episode severely damaged Tito's standing with the Soviet forces. However, the partisans were helped in September 1943 by the collapse of Italy (which enabled many Italian troops to join the partisans, forming the Garibaldi Division) and the decision by the British and the Americans in November 1943 to support Tito over Mihailović. This decision by the western Allies to support a Communist-led organization was based on one pragmatic consideration: the partisans were 'killing most Germans'. Thus, in November 1943, the KPT set up a government with Tito as Marshal and President of the National Committee for the Liberation of Yugoslavia. With the help of Soviet troops, Tito was able to install himself in Belgrade within a year, effectively destroying any remaining power held by Mihailović. Although fighting between the partisans and the Germans continued until 15 May 1945, the Communists formed a provisional government consisting of 23 Communists, 2 Communist sympathizers, and

3 non-Communists who returned from exile in London. The Allies recognized this government and subsequent elections turned Yugoslavia into a Communist regime.

The Germans Attack Greece

Meanwhile, at around the same time as the Germans were invading Yugoslavia, they attacked mainland Greece from the north. The Greek army was quickly surrounded and the British troops supporting it were forced to retreat southward. By the end of April 1941, the British had been evacuated to Crete, the Greek King had been sent into exile, and a collaborationist government had been set up under General G. Tsolakoglou. The 40,000 British, Australian, New Zealand, and Greek Allies who had been evacuated to Crete then experienced the first airborne invasion in history. On 20 May 1941, German parachutists and assault gliders descended upon Crete. Within ten days, the under-equipped Allied troops were pushed off the island. Nevertheless, the Germans paid a high price for victory: 4,000 Germans were killed and another 2,000 were wounded. One-third of the German transport aircraft used in the attack were destroyed. The Allies comforted themselves with the thought that the campaign in the Balkans had delayed the invasion of the USSR, but they also recognized that Allied prestige had been severely dented: 10,000 British, 90,000 Yugoslavian, and 270,000 Greek troops found themselves prisoners of war.

In Greece, popular resistance to the German presence was exceptionally vigorous. Acts of resistance included symbolic ones such as ripping down the Nazi flag flying over the

Acropolis and hoisting the Greek flag, establishing soup kitchens to feed the starving, or blowing up Bulgarian ships in the Piraeus harbour. Organized forms of resistance were strengthened by three factors. First, many Greek soldiers had brought their rifles back with them after their defeat in the spring of 1941. These weapons were invaluable in enabling guerrilla groups to 'pick off' isolated German units. Secondly, the Communist resistance was helped by the failure of the King and the government-in-exile to mount an effective resistance movement. Indeed, the fact that the King enjoyed lavish residence in Claridges (a luxurious hotel in London) during the war was deeply offensive to many Greeks. Finally, the grave situation in which the Greeks found themselves meant that they had little to lose by resisting. In particular, resistance was greatly stimulated by the 'winter starvation' of 1941–2, during which at least 100,000 Greeks starved to death. This was what led young women like Anthoula into the resistance. She was 12 years old when war was declared, and quickly joined the youth resistance. She recalled:

As the occupation progressed, we grew more and more hungry because in the beginning they had taken all our food. They had taken all our supplies. The first winter was absolutely tragic. People were dying of hunger. We had neither wood to heat our houses nor food to eat. The Nazis had taken all the food from the villages and either used it themselves or sent it outside the country. In the capital [Athens], where we didn't have fields or gardens, we suffered the most. And so we saw our first dead bodies, but they were people who had starved to death. The second year, however, things had changed. There were big demonstrations, organized by *E.A.M.*. And . . . We also started, from the first

> months, to write slogans on walls . . . As younger people, our
> job was to transport various things . . . Many times I would be
> carrying weapons in my schoolbag.[3]

Eventually, Anthoula was arrested by the Germans in 1944, taken to Merlin Prison, where she was tortured for several weeks, and then sent to Ravensbruck concentration camp for the rest of the war.

As Anthoula's explanation for joining the resistance suggests, the most important resistance movement was the left-wing *Ethniko Apeleftherotiko Metopo* (*EAM* or the National Liberation Front), formed in September 1941, and its military wing (known as *ELAS*), which was responsible for attacking Wehrmacht units. By 1944, they had between 1.5 and 2 million members—that is, 30 per cent of the Greek population. Like Tito, *EAM* insisted that the national liberation struggle was tied into the broader war for national independence. It promised that, after the war, *EAM* would safeguard national independence against foreign intervention. Its slogan, 'Greece for the Greeks', with its promise of empowering the poorer classes, was immensely popular. *EAM* was building upon a long-term and deep desire within Greek society for democracy.

Although they were accused of terrorizing Greek villagers, of encouraging reprisals (the Germans killed fifty locals for every German killed by a 'bandit'), and of indiscriminate executions of traitors and 'reactionaries', *EAM/ELAS* were remarkably effective. Indeed, they virtually governed much of Greece, especially in areas outside the main towns, by establishing forms of self-government in law, education, and business. They were unable to save the Jews, however, despite some efforts. Ninety-eight per cent of the Greek

Jewish population (most of whom lived in Salonika) died during the war. The almost total destruction of Greek Jews was a deliberate Nazi policy. As Colonel Rudolf Höss, Commandant of Auschwitz, said in July 1944: 'the Greek Jews were of such poor quality that they all had to be eliminated.'[4]

Despite failing to save the Jews, *EAM* was one of the strongest resistance movements on the Allied side during the war. The Greek tragedy was that after the liberation *EAM* (which was led by Communists) ended up engaged in battle with a Greek right-wing group that had the support of the British. In December 1944, the British turned against *EAM/ELAS* and active fighting broke out between the resistance and Allied troops. Churchill was determined that Communism would be routed from Greece and promised to ensure the return of the king. Support for the monarchy would guarantee continued British influence in Greece, preserving the 'imperial road' to India and to oil. Ironically, former collaborators of the Axis occupation aided the British. In the civil war that resulted, both sides committed atrocities. War in Greece did not really end until August 1949, when the Communist guerrillas were defeated. According to one estimate, half a million people were killed between 1945 and 1949. By then, the British had been replaced by the Americans, who supported the restored monarchy and controlled the post-war state. Furthermore, the civil war and its oppressive aftermath eventually led to the brutal military dictatorship of 1967 to 1974.

The Western Desert and North Africa

While the anti-fascist struggle and the civil war were raging in Greece, Mussolini had been experiencing even less success in the Western Desert (Libya and Egypt) and North Africa. In these campaigns, a very different kind of battle was required. Fierce winds—the *khamsin* and the *ghibli*—threw dust into men's faces, obscuring the battlefield. Sand clogged the equipment; the featureless terrain made navigation difficult. Nevertheless, access to the Suez Canal, a vital communications link for the Allies, was at stake. The Suez Canal linked Britain with India, halving the time it took to travel between them, and Egypt was also a convenient staging point for Allied troops travelling to the Far East and southern Europe.

In September 1940, Mussolini sent Italian troops based in Libya into British-held Egypt. It was a fiasco. British troops took less than two months to push the Italian forces from Egypt. Thirty-six thousand British troops defeated around 4 million Italians. The Italian army simply collapsed. Their men had little fighting spirit left, equipment and weapons were in short supply, and the officers were incompetent (the commanding general conducted the campaign from the safety of the Italian mainland and other officers travelled with caravans of prostitutes).

Hitler was disgusted. He was rumoured to have proposed a special medal for Italian soldiers—it was to be pinned to their backs so it would be visible in retreat. In order to turn the battle around, he sent in General Erwin Rommel to command the troops. The Afrika Korps was born, adopting the Swahili war cry: 'Heia Safari', or 'Let's go and get 'em!' Rommel possessed both panache and skill. He recognized that war in the desert shared a great deal with war at sea. Mobility was the key: the conquering army would be the one most capable of transversing vast distances quickly in order to attack the enemy. Even Churchill admitted in the House of Commons that 'We have a daring and skilful opponent against us, and, may I say across the havoc of war, a great general.' Historians disagree as to whether Rommel deserved such praise, but the legend of the 'Desert Fox' has survived all attempts of debunking.

Although Rommel brought with him a formidable reputation gained in France and a sophisticated understanding of tactics, he had to lead a hastily formed corps that lacked experience of desert warfare. The first thing he did was to insist upon close collaboration between the army, navy, and air force. Only this would enable them to cope with limited supplies and a taxing environment. He also developed a tactic that he had employed successfully in France in 1940— a gun 'line' of 88s that could rebuff Allied tanks at a distance of over three kilometres.

Despite his tactical skill and repeated victories against the Allies in mid-1941, Rommel found himself in a weak position by November. He struck back in January 1942, captured Tobruk (the Libyan port that had been under siege since the start of this campaign), and forced the British to retreat into Egypt. However, two battles at El Alamein—in July and October–November 1942—saw his armies disintegrate. On 1 November 1942, just days before the end of the second battle of El Alamein, Lieutenant-General Sir Bernard Montgomery, Commander of the British Eighth Army, wrote:

> I am fighting a terrific battle with Rommel. It began on 23

October and he is resisting desperately. I hold the initiative. But it has become a real solid and bloody killing match. I do not think he can go on much longer. I am dealing him a terrific blow in the very early hours of tomorrow 2nd Nov. and it may well be that that will knock him off his perch. I hope so . . . [5]

He reported victory within days.

Then, on 8 November 1942, 100,000 British and American troops landed in Morocco and Algeria (in French North Africa) and seized the vital ports of Algiers, Oran, and Casablanca. This was known as Operation Torch. Rommel was forced to retreat to Tripoli (the capital of Libya), where he was vastly outnumbered by Allied troops. An Allied air and sea cordon meant that Rommel's armies suffered a severe shortage of fuel, ammunition, and transport. Believing that North Africa should be abandoned, Rommel flew to East Prussia on 28 November 1942 to appeal directly to Hitler. Hitler reacted with fury, blaming Rommel for the defeat at El Alamein and accusing his troops of cowardice. *Luftwaffe* Field Marshal Erhard Milch later recorded in his diary how Rommel 'buried his head in my shoulder and wept for some time. He just couldn't get over Hitler's lack of trust in his leadership.'[6] Back in the desert, the Axis offensives faltered. Surrender came just six months later, on 13 May 1943. It had taken three years of fighting before the Afrika Korps was defeated and the war in North Africa was over.

The defeat of the Afrika Korps was a brutal blow to the Axis powers. Hitler had lost 250,000 men, and Italy and Nazi-occupied Europe were now vulnerable. In Germany, the defeat was particularly demoralizing, coming as it did so soon after the German failure at Stalingrad (described in the next chapter). But, in the end, what was achieved? For the Allies, the campaign was necessary to protect the sea passage to the Middle East—and the Middle East meant oil, without which the war would be quickly decided. From another point of view, however, the entire campaign was a sideshow. Hitler was more focused on the USSR and the Americans were keen to cross the Channel and defeat Germany in France and then in Germany itself. One historian has likened the campaign to the answer given by a mountain climber when asked why he climbed a particular mountain: 'Because it is there.' The Allies fought the Italians and Germans in the deserts of Libya, Egypt, and North Africa 'because they were there'.

Rommel's war continued. He went on to serve his Führer in Normandy but was implicated in the July 1944 plot to kill Hitler. In order to protect his family from persecution, he chose to commit suicide. In the desert, he had fought a chivalrous war; he died in a similar fashion.

Italian Occupation and Liberation

When the Americans joined the Allies, the Italian public was dismayed. It had never been wholeheartedly behind the war in the first place and its ties to America were strong as a result of mass emigration to the USA since the late nineteenth century. As a consequence, when Allied troops landed in Sicily on 10 July 1943, the Italian people heralded them as liberators. This Allied invasion was the greatest amphibious assault of the war, involving half a million troops landing on the island despite high winds and rough seas. Eighty thousand German and Italian troops were captured and, within a month, the Allies claimed victory. This time, Hitler did not come to Mussolini's aid. Mussolini was removed from office and replaced by the 72-year-old Badoglio, who signed an armistice with the Allies on 3 September 1943.

It was already too late. Germany invaded Italy, allegedly on the grounds of helping the Italians fight in case of an Allied invasion but really for strategic reasons and because Germany needed Italy's industrial resources. In September, Hitler set Mussolini up as a puppet ruler in northern Italy. Partisan groups—largely led by the Communist Party and the Action Party—quickly developed, leading to a savage civil war between the anti-fascists and Mussolini's supporters in the north. In September 1943, there were 25,000 active resistance fighters in Italy, a number that grew to 250,000 (including around 55,000 female partisans) by April 1945. As elsewhere, the cost of resistance was high. For every act of sabotage, innocent people were killed, most notoriously in the massacre of 335 Italians at the Ardeatine caves (near Rome) on 24 March 1944 in reprisal for the success of Roman partisans in blowing up thirty-two German military police. When Allied armies entered northern Italy in October 1944, Mussolini tried to flee with his mistress, Clara Petacci. However, they were captured by partisans and shot. Their bodies were thrown into a truck, taken to Milan, and strung up by their heels in the square for all to jeer at.

The process of pushing the Germans out of Italy was a slow one, and painful for the participants. Lieutenant Walter F. Commander was from Buffalo, New York, but his tearful letter to his wife on 3 June 1944 could have been written by a combatant on any side of the conflict. He wrote:

My Dearest Dolly,

That I cannot write more often in these trying days is a constant thorn in my side ... My constant thought is: this letter may be the one she reads just before the baby comes ... My darling, things are a little better with me now. Hellishly, one can get hardened to the sights and smells of the battle-field. Only in the back of the brain a voice repeats: this is unnatural and not a part of life. And all of the consciousness returns to the reality of your miracle—there is no death in that ... Will there ever be a peace for me? I want to remain changeless for you, Dolly, but I can see the changes in myself even as the days pass. You get something twisted out of your insides by all this filth and sewage ... Darling, hold me so close tonight. Never before have I had so much need of you. I love you.[7]

He was killed in action in Italy only thirteen days later. The Italian war ended in May 1945. As in Greece, Italy's long agony was only officially over. In Italy, a state of near civil war began, as ex-fascists were hunted out and killed by partisans. One conservative estimate puts the number killed in this way at over 2,300, while others claim the numbers summarily executed may have been as high as 30,000. This remains an extremely controversial subject in popular Italian politics.

As with the other campaigns, questions were asked as to whether it was necessary for the Allies to devote so many troops to the Italian theatre. The Allies claimed to be 'striking at the soft underbelly' of the Axis, and the campaigns did keep German forces committed in the Mediterranean. Even Hitler admitted, after the Allied invasion of Italy, that: 'It is in fact quite obvious that our Italian alliance has been of more service to our enemies than to ourselves ... If, in spite of all our efforts, we fail to win this war, the Italian alliance will have contributed to our defeat.'[8] In Yugoslavia, Greece, and Italy, as in other countries during these dark years, the 'world war' was inextricably tied to civil war. Second only to the slaughter of the Jews, this was the true disaster of these years. Nevertheless, at the same time as battle was raging in the Balkans, the desert, and Italy, a tragedy out of all proportion to this was developing further east. As we shall see in the next chapter, the battles on the Eastern Front were in a completely different league with respect to the troops involved, the number of casualties, and the atrocities committed.

8

The Eastern Front

Annihilation and liquidation: no two words better encapsulate the war on the Eastern Front. Of all campaigns during the Second World War, this was the most bitter. Hitler intended it to be so. In a speech on 30 March 1941, he predicted that

> The war against Russia will be such that it cannot be conducted in a knightly fashion; the struggle is one of ideologies and racial differences and will have to be conducted with unprecedented, unmerciful and unrelenting harshness ... German soldiers guilty of breaking international law ... will be excused. Russia has not participated in the Hague Convention [which set out the laws of warfare] and therefore has no rights under it.

From the start, both Hitler and Joseph Goebbels (the Minister of Propaganda) recognized that the war in the east would be criminal. As Goebbels told Hitler just before the attack on 22 June 1941: 'If we emerge victorious, who will inquire as to our methods? We are already so deeply into all this that we must win; otherwise, our entire people will be eradicated.' Murderous intentions; murderous outcomes. The death rate in this campaign was astounding. While one in every 150 British soldiers was killed during the Second World War, one in every 22 Russian soldiers on the Eastern Front was killed. Of the 55 million people killed throughout the world in the Second World War, at least one-third were Russians. In fact, the horrifying fury of depravity unleashed by the war in the east was much worse than this. As we shall see in the next chapter, the Holocaust can legitimately be said to have sprung from the eastern campaign.

Operation Barbarossa

For Hitler, it was axiomatic that Germany had to expand eastwards if his dream of an 'Aryan' superpower was to be realized. He believed that speedy action was necessary in order to prevent what he saw as a grave threat—that is, that the 'subhuman' Slavic races would eventually outnumber the Aryans. From the start, the war against the Soviet Union aimed to exterminate 'Jewish-Bolshevism'. German expansion and industry also required the labour and resources of this vast area. This was indeed Hitler's chief aim when he moved to conquer Norway and France in 1940. The threat from the west had to be neutralized before the conquest of the east could begin. This plan was foiled, however, when Churchill refused to negotiate a peace with Germany after the fall of France in June 1940.

Operation Barbarossa was launched at 3 a.m. on 22 June 1941. It opened along a 2,000-kilometre front and involved 140 combat divisions and 3.5 million men. As German troops fanned out in three directions—towards Leningrad, Moscow, and Kiev—Stalin was caught unawares. He had not believed that the Germans would attack, at least not at that time. Once Stalin had been forced to admit his error, his response was uncompromising. On 3 July 1941, he called upon his people to 'struggle without mercy' in the pursuit of this great 'patriotic war'. This was 'total war' as never seen before, involving the entire economy. Even women—80,000 of them—were enlisted as armed fighters in the Soviet military.

Nevertheless, the war did not start well for Stalin. Throughout 1941, the German army swept through Soviet-held territory and the Soviet Union itself. As the Soviet forces retreated, they adopted a 'scorched-earth policy', destroying houses, fuel, and property. In the front lines, the Red Army crumbled under the onslaught and the millions of Soviet troops who were taken prisoner along the way were treated with brutality. They were not regarded as 'comrades in arms' but as 'useless mouths to feed'. Prisoners were simply murdered on the spot, while those who survived the initial capture were starved or worked to death, or exposed to fatal diseases like typhus. Between 3 and 4 million Soviet prisoners of war died in captivity. That is, at least 60 per cent of Soviet POWs died in captivity (this compares with just over one-third of British and American POWs dying in captivity).

Even more cruelly, German troops targeted not only military personnel, but civilians as well. Mass killings of civilians include the Nazi massacre of 176,000 civilians in Kerch, in the Ukraine (see Figure 12). Of the 20–30 million Soviet inhabitants killed, half were civilians. German troops needed to live off the country if their advances were to continue. In such circumstances, the peasants were exploited and made to suffer. Entire towns were razed to the ground; women and

12 'Grief, Kerch, 1942': the aftermath of a Nazi massacre of civilians at Kerch, in the Ukraine (photograph by the Soviet photographer, Dmitri Baltermants)

children were massacred *en masse*. Even greater horrors were to come. The Commissar Order of 6 June 1941 ordered German troops to shoot all Red Army Commissars and Jews. In the minds of many soldiers, the two groups were identical. As one German non-commissioned officer explained in a letter to his father in July 1942: 'The great task given us in the struggle against Bolshevism, lies in the destruction of eternal Jewry. Once one sees what the Jew has done in Russia, one can well understand why the Führer began the struggle against Jewry. What sorrows would have come to our homeland, had this beast of a man had the upper hand?'[1]

Much of the killing was carried out by special units of the German SS (Security Service), called the *Einsatzgruppen*. These SS personnel and police units, aided in many cases by the regular army, ruthlessly slaughtered Communists and, above all, Jews behind the front lines. Local anti-Semites were encouraged to mount spontaneous massacres of their own. Initially, the victims were beaten to death or shot into mass graves, but, by the spring of 1942, they were being gassed in death camps: gas was considered a more efficient way of murdering large numbers of people, but it was also less psychologically difficult for the perpetrators. But that is the subject of the next chapter.

Gradually, however, the Soviet troops began turning the fight around. German brutality combined with developing nationalist spirit and a reorganization of the Red Army began to have an effect. In military terms, the most decisive battles occurred at Leningrad, Moscow, Stalingrad, and Kursk. Leningrad was a protracted campaign, but Hitler was determined to conquer the city, since he regarded it as 'the breeding centre of Bolshevism'. The German army surrounded

Leningrad on 8 September 1941. The resulting siege was to see one million Leningraders die of starvation and shells. Those who survived were brutalized: murder and cannibalism were not unknown. This trauma lasted until the city was freed on 27 January 1944.

Moscow had been attacked in October 1941, just one month after Leningrad's siege had started. Operation Typhoon, as it was called, was Hitler's attempt to subdue this great city. He decreed that 'not one Russian soldier, nor a single inhabitant—man, woman, or child—will be able to escape, and any attempt to do so will be suppressed by force'.[2] The German forces dedicated everything to this attack, but their men were exhausted, supplies were inadequate, and the Soviet troops proved particularly keen to safeguard the city. It was only the desperate reorganization of the Soviet military, combined with improvements in command and a Herculean effort by the Soviet population, that enabled the tide to turn. The fact that Stalin remained in Moscow during the battle was an immense boost to Soviet morale. Cries of 'Stalin is with us' could be heard in the streets. When the Red Army counter-attacked in December 1941, the Germans were driven out of Moscow.

It was near Moscow that 18-year-old Zoya Kosmodemyanskaya (see Figure 13) was hanged in early December 1941. She had been in the tenth form of school when the war began, loved *War and Peace*, and was an avid reader of Chekhov. Before her death for resistance activities, she was tortured so severely that even some of her torturers felt sick.

While Leningrad and Moscow were under siege, Stalingrad was attacked (see Figure 14). For Hitler, Stalingrad was important, because he needed to protect the Romanian

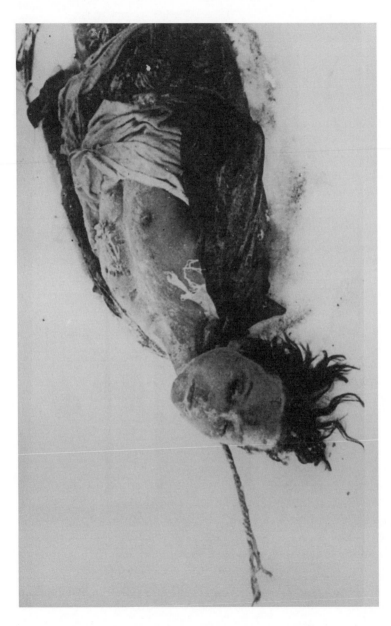

13 'Zoya Kosmodemyanskaya, Tania': a partisan tortured to death by the Germans (photograph by Serguei Strunnikov)

oilfields, upon which his entire campaign in the east depended. This battle lasted from August 1942 until February 1943, with the Red Army gaining ground only from November 1942 when they surrounded the German 6th Army. German commanders on the ground urged a quick break-out, but Hitler ordered them to stay where they were and engage the Red Army from a defensive position. Hitler intended to supply the trapped soldiers from the air. The 6th Army would have needed food, ammunition, and other provisions weighing between 1,600 and 2,600 tons a day. But the Commander-in-Chief of the *Luftwaffe*, Reichsmarschall Hermann Göring, was asked to fly in only 300 tons a day. In the end, the daily average of supplies was only 100 tons. Before the end of the year, the trapped German troops were dying of malnutrition, hypothermia, and diseases such as typhoid, typhus, and dysentery. On 10 January 1943, when the Germans again refused to surrender, the Red Army struck in what became the bloodiest battle of the entire war. Ninety-nine per cent of Stalingrad was destroyed. Of the 500,000 inhabitants of the city, only 1,500 remained after the battle. Military casualties were also high, on both sides. Half a million Soviet troops were killed, along with more than 150,000 German and Romanian soldiers. Even after the fighting had ended, the dying continued. Of the 91,000 Germans captured at Stalingrad, more than 50,000 died of starvation and exposure within a month. Hitler's 6th Army had been utterly destroyed. In the words of General Siegfried Westphal, 'never before in Germany's history has so large a body of troops come to so dreadful an end'.[3]

Despite these bitter defeats, there was one decisive battle to come. On the vast plains of central Russia, the Germans

14 Street fighting in Stalingrad, 1942

launched 'Operation Citadel', or the Battle of Kursk. Hitler was keen for victory here, since it would enable him to destroy two Russian fronts in one battle. He also believed that it was a favourable time to attack. The Allies had not invaded France as he had expected (leaving Hitler with some reserve troops) and he believed that the German panzer forces were superior to those of the Russians. For the German army, 'Operation Citadel' was an opportunity to take revenge for the humiliating defeat at Moscow (1941) and Stalingrad (1942). The battle lasted fifty days, from 5 July to 23 August 1943, and engaged more tanks, mortars, guns, and aircraft than any other battle of the Second World War. It engaged one-third of all the German divisions on the Eastern Front. It was a pincer attack in which the two German 'wedges'—from Oryol-Kursk and Belgorod-Kharkov—were sent to enclose and conquer the 'Kursk bulge', an area of 65,000 kilometres still held by Soviet troops. Again, the Germans had gambled on a rapid victory and, when this did not occur, they were unprepared for a battle of attrition. At Kursk, the Red Army proved its superior mobility. While the Germans were dependent upon the railroad to transport their divisions, the Russians were able to move their men by trucks. This use of the roads gave the Red Army speed and greater flexibility. The Red Army was also able to replace the tanks it lost in the fighting much more rapidly than the Germans. In the end, Hitler called off the campaign, frightened by news that the western Allies had landed in Sicily and that Italy was preparing to pull out of the war. German troops were desperately needed in the Mediterranean.

The defeat of the Germans at Kursk was crushing. It placed them in a defensive position, gave the initiative to the Soviets, and shattered German morale. After that, the premonition of defeat tormented German army personnel. In the words of Colonel-General Heinz Guderian, Germany's Chief of Army General Staff between 1944 and 1945: 'Needless to say, the Russians exploited their victory to the full. There were to be no more periods of quiet on the Eastern Front. From now on the enemy was in undisputed possession.'[4] A 21-year-old Italian second-lieutenant, Eugenio Corti, was one of the 30,000 Italians who fought with the Germans on the Eastern Front. After the defeat, he dedicated a book of his memoirs to his dead comrades:

> For those who shared those days with me,
> Who fought and suffered with me,
> Who hoped so desperately with me,
> And in the end remained lifeless
> On the interminable roads of the steppe.[5]

The Battle of Kursk signalled the beginning of the end of the war on the Eastern Front.

Soviet Victory

In this struggle of the two titans, what enabled the Soviets to win? Hitler had expected the Soviet army to fold as easily as every other European nation had done. His early victories seemed to confirm his belief that this was going to be a short war lasting six weeks. Hitler had once famously said of the Russians: 'We only have to kick in the door and the whole rotten structure will come crashing down.' Rule number one in war: never underestimate your opponent. Rule number

15 Russian cartoon by Koukrinikci. The Russian text says, 'Napoleon suffered defeat. The same thing will happen to Hitler'

two, as Napoleon learned: never invade Russia. Hitler referred frequently to Napoleon in the campaign, but failed to heed this warning (see Figure 15).

Initially at least certain weaknesses of the Soviet forces gave an advantage to Hitler's armies. The Red Army had grown exceptionally quickly, from only 940,000 men in 1936 to nearly 5 million by 1941. Soviet troops were poorly trained and disciplined. They were handicapped by the wide gap between senior and junior offices and a general atmosphere of secrecy and fear within the army and the Party. The purges immediately prior to the war had not helped. Between 1937 and 1939, Stalin had purged three out of five marshals, thirteen out of fifteen army commanders, and all the military district commanders in office in May 1937, in addition to the leading officers in the navy and air force. He had also imprisoned or executed 35,000 officers. Nevertheless, the myth of the invincible Red Army led to an underestimation of its opponent's strength and to severe demoralization after defeat. Finally, the Soviets' problems extended well beyond the military apparatus: as late as 1941, Soviet industry was still incapable of producing sufficient quantities of munitions for such a war.

These weaknesses were dwarfed by the problems facing the invading Germans. Their chief problem was keeping their lines of supply open. They lacked fuel. Stalin had superior equipment, particularly the T-34 tank. Roads were impassible, owing to rain and mud. Hitler had not planned for a long war. He was hampered by the fact that Russian factories and populations had been transferred from the war zone in the west. One-eighth of industry had been relocated in the Urals, Central Asia, and Siberia. The Germans had few reserves in manpower or material. Huge losses could not be replaced. The distances the troops were expected to travel were immense. For instance, it was more than 1,000 kilometres from the USSR's western border to Moscow. This distance had to be traversed in particularly severe climatic conditions. While the Red Army wore felt boots, fur caps, and winter garments, the German soldiers were poorly dressed. They had no winter uniforms and the small number of Italian troops had shoes made from cardboard. Hundreds of thousands suffered frostbite; their rifles and guns froze up and they suffered from dysentery. For instance, in the battle for Moscow in November 1941, temperatures dropped as low as −56°C and temperatures of between −20 and −30°C were not uncommon. 'General Winter' was a powerful ally of the Russians.

Resistance

More fundamentally, Hitler had underestimated the resistance of the state and its people. Soviet troops turned out to possess immense reservoirs of endurance. The resistance of partisans was also decisive. The German army was ill prepared to deal with guerrilla attacks and in response to casualties it lashed out with violent reprisals. The Barbarossa Directive of 13 May 1941 ordered troops to shoot anyone who offered resistance. Thus, in one month alone during the terrible autumn of 1941, the 707th Infantry Division killed over 10,000 alleged partisans. It was made worse on 16 September 1941, when Wilhelm Keitel (Commander in Chief of Germany's armed forces from 1938 to 1945 and the instrument through which Hitler ran the war) ordered the killing of between 50 and 100 Communists for every German killed by a partisan.

Of course, the partisan movement developed only slowly. Many people in the areas occupied by the Germans recalled the forced collectivization of agriculture under the Communists and the murder of their cultural leaders. At first, many welcomed the German invaders for rescuing them from Stalin. Disillusionment settled in quickly. The gross brutality of SS murder squads fuelled partisan activity. As a report submitted by the German Ministry of Propaganda was forced to admit, the attitude of the people in occupied areas was: 'If I stay with the Germans, I will be killed by the Bosheviks when they come. Should the Bolsheviks not come, I'll get killed by the Germans sooner or later. Therefore, staying with the Germans means certain death, joining the partisans most probably salvation.'[6] By early 1942, 150,000 partisans were actively engaging with the German occupiers. Within two years, over 250,000 men and women were fighting as partisans. Male and female partisans ambushed German personnel, disrupted lines of transport and communication, and generally made life unpleasant by constant harassment. Their actions were particularly good at distracting German troops from other activities. According to one estimate, the German army was forced to devote 10 per cent of its manpower to combating the partisans.

Ina Konstantinova was one Russian who fought as a partisan from the age of 16. She heard the radio announcement by Vyachlesav Molotov (the Soviet Foreign Minister) that the Soviet Union had been attacked. As she recorded in her diary on 22 June 1941:

Only yesterday everything was so peaceful, so quiet, and today ... my God! At noon we heard Molotov's speech broadcasted [*sic*] over the radio: Germany is bombing our nation, and German bombs have fallen on Kiev, Zhitamir, and other Ukraine cities. The country is endangered. I can't describe my state of mind as I was listening to this speech! I became so agitated that my heart seemed about to jump out. The country is mobilizing; could I continue as before? No! I ought to make myself useful to my homeland, to the best of my ability, in its hour of need. We must win![7]

She worked as a spy and a saboteur behind German lines and

was personally responsible for killing fifteen Germans before being shot herself at the age of 17.

Revenge

A combination of superior tactics, better use of material, and fierce military and partisan fighting led to Soviet victory. After the German defeat at Stalingrad, the chase was resumed in the other direction, as German troops were gradually pushed out of Soviet territory. In their pursuit of their German foe, the Red Army participated in mass atrocities. Some of the worst atrocities were committed in the Ukraine and Belorussia. In these territories, violence erupted even before the Red Army arrived. The collapse of the Polish administration meant that simmering ethnic and economic hatreds rose to the surface. Poles, Polish Pans (or the *beloruchki*, 'those with white hands'), were viciously attacked by peasants and workers, on the grounds that, as capitalists and landholders, they were class enemies. In the streets, one slogan reverberated: 'For Poles, Pans, and dogs—a dog's death.'[8] The Red Army sanctioned the actions of bands of vigilantes.

As Soviet soldiers moved westwards and into German territory, they wreaked a terrible revenge. The tone was set at the first German village they encountered. This was Nemmersdorf in East Prussia. Soviet troops entered the village on 22 October 1944 and raped, mutilated, and killed all the women. Some of the victims were sawn in half. They cut off the genitals of the male POWs and Polish workers in the village. Similar scenes of brutality were rehearsed throughout Soviet-occupied Germany. Konstantin Simonev's poem sums up the mood:

> Kill a German, kill him soon
> And every time you see one—kill him!

When Soviet troops conquered Berlin in May 1945 after long, bloody months of battle, looting, murder, and rape by the occupying forces became part of everyday life for Berliners. Some indication of the terror of German women can be seen in one brutal statistic: in certain districts of Berlin, women's suicide rate rose to 215 per 1,000. Aleksandr Solzhenitsyn's poem *Prussian Nights* depicts the personal devastation in this desperate city:

> A moaning, by the walls half muffled:
> The mother's wounded, still alive.
> The little daughter's on the mattress,
> Dead. How many have been on it?
> A platoon, a company perhaps?
> A girl's been turned into a woman,
> A woman turned into a corpse.
> It's all come down to simple phrases:
> Do not forget! Do not forgive!
> *Blood for blood!* A tooth for a tooth!
> The mother begs, 'Töte mich, Soldat!' (Kill me, soldier.)[9]

None of this was admitted by the Soviet administration. At the end of the war, Stalin made his speech of victory: 'My dear fellow countrymen and women. I am proud today to call you my comrades. Your courage has defeated the Nazis. The age-long struggle of the Slav nations for their existence and independence has ended in victory. The war is over. Now we shall build a Russia fit for heroes and heroines.'[10]

The Red Army had been victorious, but the cost had been high for both sides. Between 1941 and 1945, 10 million Soviet soldiers had been killed, many through illness and deprivation. At least 10 million Soviet citizens were killed. There was no more terrible campaign in the entire war, but this chapter tells only a small part of the terror. Another, even worse, story has to be told.

9

The Holocaust

At the same time as Operation Barbarossa was beginning, the mass killing of the Jews started. Indeed, this was not a coincidence, since Bolshevism and the Jewish threat were merged in Hitler's mind. It was on the Eastern Front that the systematic slaughter of Jews began and from there that it then spread to the rest of Europe. The horror of this event in history lies in the calculated nature of the slaughter, in the number of people killed and implicated in the killing, and the grotesque ideological and material infrastructure employed in the attempt to carry out the mass murder of an entire people. Approximately 6 million Jews were killed, including around 2 million children. Between one-third and one-half of all the Jews killed were Soviet Jews. However, although Jews were the central targets for genocide, other ethnic, social, religious, political, and sexual minorities were also singled out for severe repression and 'elimination'. Furthermore, not all the executioners were Germans. Wherever they went, the conquering German forces were aided and abetted in their crimes by local collaborators.

One Victim

The words of one of the victims may be used to convey some of the incomprehensibility of the Holocaust. We don't know the woman's name, but simply that she was killed in the Tarnopol Ghetto along with the rest of the 500,000-strong community of Galician Jews. Her letters were found in May 1943 amongst a pile of clothing taken from a group of victims. These are her letters:

7 April 1943. Before I leave this world, I want to leave behind a few lines to you, my loved ones. When this letter reaches you one day, I myself will no longer be there, nor will any of us. Our end is drawing near. One feels it, one knows it. Just like the innocent, defenceless Jews already executed, we are all condemned to death. In the very near future it will be our turn, as the small remainder left over from the mass murders. There is no way for us to escape this horrible, ghastly death. At the very beginning (in June 1941) some 5000 men were killed, among them my husband. After six weeks, following a five-day search between the corpses, I found his body ... Since that day, life has ceased for me. Not even in my girlish dreams could I once have wished for a better and more faithful companion. I was only granted two years and two months of happiness. And now? Tired from so much searching among the bodies, one was 'glad' to have found his as well; are there words in which to express these torments?

26 April 1943. I am still alive and I want to describe to you what happened from the 7th to this day. Now then, it is told that everyone's turn comes up next. Galicia should be totally rid of Jews. After all, the ghetto is to be liquidated by the 1st of May. During the last days thousands have been shot. Meeting-

point was in our camp. Here the human victims are selected. In Petrikow it looks like this: before the grave one is stripped naked, then forced to kneel down and wait for the shot. The victims stand in line and await their turn. Moreover, they have to sort the first, the executed, in their graves so that the space is used well and order prevails. The entire procedure does not take long. In half an hour the clothes of the executed return to the camp. After the actions the Jewish council received a bill for 30,000 Zloty to pay for used bullets . . . Why can we not cry, why can we not defend ourselves? How can one see so much innocent blood flow and say nothing, do nothing and await the same death oneself? We are compelled to go under so miserably, so pitilessly . . . Do you think we want to end this way, die this way? No! No! Despite all these experiences. The urge for self-preservation has now often become greater, the will to live stronger, the closer death is. It is beyond comprehension.[1]

Those last words—'It is beyond comprehension'—haunt any discussion of the Holocaust.

Nazism

How could this have happened? The persecution of the Jews did not begin with the war but had a history that went back for centuries. In the late 1890s, anti-Semitism became racial rather than religious. It was central to the ideology of Nazism. The Nazis became the largest political party in July 1932 when they won 37 per cent of the vote, the most they ever achieved in a free election. Anti-Semitism was not the main reason for the Nazi victory. The Nazis presented themselves as the party most likely to offer political stability and economic prosperity during a period of prolonged crisis. Nevertheless, anti-Semitism was rife in German society. The Jews were seen by many as embodying every anti-German value. National Socialism tapped into this widely held belief. As Rudolf Hess (deputy leader of the Nazi Party until his dramatic surrender to the British in May 1941) argued, National Socialism could best be described as 'applied biology'. According to this view, the 'Aryan race' was superior. The Jews were blamed for all of Germany's ills, including Germany's defeat in the First World War and the so-called bolshevization of Germany's cultural life. Nazi caricatures of the Jews were dramatically represented in the film *The Eternal Jew* (1940), in which Jews were portrayed as similar to rats or parasites, spreading disease and disorder wherever they went.

From 1933, when Hitler became the leader of a one-party state, measures against Jews, Gypsies, homosexuals, the mentally and physically handicapped, and other 'undesirables' were introduced. In 1933, a law was passed enforcing the compulsory sterilization of anyone suffering from a supposedly hereditary disease (including alcoholism and 'moral feeble-mindedness'). Under the 'Third Reich', about 400,000 people were sterilized under the law. Two years later, it was expanded to allow for compulsory abortion in cases of pregnancy amongst women suffering a hereditary disease. Another law barred Jews from the professions and the civil service. A most significant moment came in 1935, when the Nuremberg Laws stripped German Jews of their German citizenship and outlawed marriage and sexual relations between Jewish and non-Jewish Germans. In total, the Third Reich passed 400 anti-Jewish laws. A turning point was *Kristallnacht*, or the 'Night of Broken Glass', on the night of 9–10 November 1938. It was a full-scale pogrom during which Nazis arrested 20,000 Jews and sent them to concentration camps for a brief period. Many Jews were murdered and their homes and businesses destroyed and over 1,000 synagogues were razed to the ground. After *Kristallnacht*, the remaining Jewish retail businesses and industrial enterprises were quickly 'Aryanized' or liquidated.

Against such a background, it is hardly surprising that about half the Jewish population of Germany emigrated before war was declared. With the onset of war, however, the stakes were raised dramatically, in part because the 'Greater German Reich' had now conquered Poland and, with it, well over 2 million Jews who lived there. If the first phase of the Holocaust involved large-scale discrimination against and isolation of Jews, the second phase involved plans to deport Jews to 'Jewish reservations' in the conquered Polish territories, in Madagascar (a plan never actually put into effect), and in the Soviet Union. This 'territorial solution' was intended to lead to the total destruction of European Jewry after the war. Already from the invasion of Poland in September 1939, many thousands of Polish Jews had been shot or herded into overcrowded and unsanitary ghettos. In June 1941, the SS 'task forces' followed the German army into Soviet territory, systematically shooting hundreds of thousands of Jewish men, women, and children

The 'Final Solution'

By this time, extreme levels of persecution and mass murder had already become a fully integrated part of the Nazi political system. The systematic slaughter of Poles and POWs on the Eastern Front has already been mentioned. In addition, Nazi 'racial science' classified Sinti and Roma ('Gypsies') as *Untermenschen* or 'subhumans'. Along with the Jews, measures were passed that progressively stripped them of all civil rights. From 1933, Sinti, Roma, and 'beggars' were rounded up and moved to isolated camps, where they could be studied and used as cheap labour. These camps—known as *Zigeunerlager*—were visited by officers from the Office for Research on Race, Hygiene, and Population Biology (part of the Board of Health), who registered the Sinti and Roma according to race and genealogy. The definition of 'Gypsy' was wide: if two of an individual's sixteen great-grandparents were Roma or Sinti, that individual was classified as 'Gypsy-mixture' and, from 1943 onwards, could be deported to concentration camps such as Auschwitz-Birkenau, Buchenwald, and Ravensbrück. Between one-quarter and one-third of Sinti and Roma living in Europe were killed by the Nazis.

Male homosexuals were also targeted. Heinrich Himmler (the head of the SS and the Gestapo) estimated that 10 per cent of German males were homosexuals and, since he believed that they were betraying the 'Ayran race' by refusing to procreate, they had to be killed. Male homosexuals were rounded up and sent to camps (most frequently to Sachsenhausen and Buchenwald), where they were forced to wear pink triangles while being worked to death. When labour shortages were particularly desperate, a homosexual could barter his freedom by allowing himself to be castrated or by having sex with a prostitute. By doing this, though, he exchanged back-breaking labour combined with torture in a camp for back-breaking labour in a factory. Lesbians did not suffer the same decree of persecution. After all, as Himmler quipped, 'lesbians can give birth'.

The mass murder of people who were mentally ill or physically handicapped had also taken place before 1941. As early as 1924, Hitler wrote in *Mein Kampf* that making it 'impossible for mentally deficient people to beget equally deficient offspring is the demand of a healthy understanding, and a purposeful campaign to this end would signify the most humane act imaginable'. In October 1939, he commissioned certain doctors to perform 'mercy deaths' on patients judged to be incurably mentally or physically ill or handicapped. In the end, the 'euthanasia' programme resulted in the slaughter of around 200,000.

So, the 'Final Solution' for Jews grew out of a political system that was already comfortable with the idea and act of mass murder. Although Hitler's extermination of the Jews was well under way by the end of 1941, it was at the Wannsee Conference on 20 January 1942 that Reinhard Heydrich, head of the Reich Security Office, officially announced the Nazi programme of eliminating all Jews. This meeting took place in the Berlin suburb of Wannsee, where fifteen SS officers and government officials came together to coordinate the 'Final Solution'. It was decreed that most Jews would be sent eastwards to engage in forced labour, during which 'a great part will undoubtedly be eliminated by natural causes'. Since those who survived would be the strongest, they represented the greatest threat to the Nazis and would have to be 'treated accordingly'. The morality of killing all Jews was barely questioned. The only topic that caused debate was what should happen to those of 'mixed blood': should they be killed or merely sterilized? The entire conference took less than two hours.

From 1939 and above all since June 1941, Jews, Communists, 'Gypsies', and other 'undesirables' were rounded up and exterminated by mass shootings in or near burial pits (see Figure 16). This caused emotional trauma for some perpetrators. For instance, the German soldier, August Zorn, was present at the massacre at Zózefów in Poland in July 1942 when 1,800 Jews were rounded up, the healthy men were sent to a camp at Lublin and the old men, women, and children were killed. Zorn was ordered to kill a very old man. In his words, the man

> could not or would not keep up with his countrymen, because he repeatedly fell and then simply lay there. I regularly had to lift him up and drag him forward. Thus, I only reached the execution site when my comrades had already shot their Jews. At the sight of his countrymen who had been shot, my Jew threw himself on the ground and remained lying there. I then cocked by carbine and shot him through the back of the head. Because I was already very upset from the cruel treatment of the Jews during the clearing of the town and was completely in turmoil, I shot too high. The entire back of the skull of my Jew was torn off and the brain exposed. Parts of the skull flew into Sergeant Steinmetz's face. This was grounds for me, after returning to the truck, to go to the first sergeant and ask for my release. I had become so sick that I simply couldn't anymore.[2]

Because some men like Zorn had difficulty with such face-to-

16 A group of Jewish women, some with babies in their arms, before their execution in Misocz, Ukraine, 14 October 1942. Local collaborators are shown assisting the Germans

face encounters, some officers began experimenting with gas. Mobile gas vans had been in operation since December 1941, killing up to sixty people at a time by carbon monoxide poisoning. One eyewitness recalled:

> They drove into the prison yard and the Jews, men, women, and children, had to climb into the vans directly from their cells. I am also familiar with the interior of the vans. They had metal fittings and a wooden grating on top. The exhaust fumes were fed into the interior of the van. Even today I can hear the knocking, the screaming of the Jews: 'dear Germans, let us out.'[3]

But this was inefficient and could be carried out only on a small scale. It was slow, and some people were found to be still alive when the doors were opened. Hence, the highly toxic gas Zyklon B was proposed. It was initially designed for the extermination of lice and was cheap and easy to use. Within five minutes of contact, it was fatal. Zyklon B was used in the gas chambers at the concentration camp in Auschwitz. After death, the bodies were robbed of everything of value, including their hair and gold teeth, and then cremated. The snow of human ash covered the countryside and towns near to the camps.

While camps such as Auschwitz-Birkenau, Belzec, Chelmno, Majdanek, Sobibor, and Treblinka were designed primarily to murder, care was taken to hide their purpose. Thus, at Treblinka (a camp designed to kill as many Jews as possible in the most efficient manner) gas chambers were disguised as mass showers. At Auschwitz, 150 miles from Warsaw, 1.1 million Jews, Russian POWs, and 'Gypsies' were killed. Pollo R. was taken there and branded with the number Z9024 (the 'Z' referred to *Zigeuner*, or 'Gypsy'). He recalled:

> Longingly I looked at the gate which barred my way out of the compound filled with screaming humanity. Near me on several trucks were hundreds of nude men, women, and children. Although they had not been on my transport, like me they were Gypsies, only they were from Silesia. I could hear and understand their prayers in Romany. They implored God (but in vain) to spare at least their children's lives. I was only fourteen at the time, and now realize that I had no real understanding of the situation I was witnessing. But instinctively I knew that something unimaginable was going to happen.
>
> We were told to line up quickly. Those that lagged a bit were hit with batons. One SS guard barked at us as he pointed toward the chimney stacks which seemed to reach for the sky like long threatening fingers, 'This will be *your* way out of Auschwitz!'[4]

The words of a 'Gypsy' song express this sentiment: 'they took us in through the gate, they let us out through the chimneys.'

In addition to these death camps, other concentration camps aimed at breaking down the prisoners both physically and psychologically. They included places like Belsen, Dachau, and Buchenwald. Many of the inmates were German Communists and other opponents of the regime. Finally, there were many labour camps, like Mittelbau-Dora in Germany where the V2 rockets were built. Thousands of slave labourers died in these camps through a combination of hard work and appalling conditions. Map 3 shows the location of the main labour, concentration, and extermination camps.

Some of the camps were used as sites for human

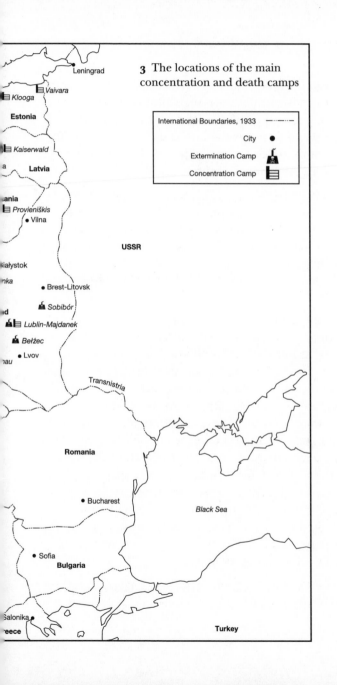

3 The locations of the main concentration and death camps

International Boundaries, 1933	— ⋅ — ⋅ —
City	●
Extermination Camp	
Concentration Camp	

Leningrad

Klooga　Vaivara

Estonia

Kaiserwald

Latvia

ania

Provieniškis

● Vilna

USSR

iałystok

nka

● Brest-Litovsk

Sobibór

Lublin-Majdanek

Bełżec

● Lvov

au

Transnistria

Romania

● Bucharest

Black Sea

● Sofia

Bulgaria

Salonika ●

eece

Turkey

experimentation. These experiments included the testing of biological weapons, sterilization, high-altitude tests, genetic manipulation, organ transplantations, and the collection of skeletons. Sinti and Roma women were also a main target for programmes of mass sterilization. 'Mrs. W.' had been sent to the 'Gypsy Block' at Auschwitz. She recalled:

> It was then said: 'The Sinti are all sterilised, so there will be no offspring.' From girls of twelve up to forty-five year olds, I will never forget it. . . . They had sterilised all the Sinti. Without anaesthetic, without anything. There were also twelve year old children. Then they took the children out in wheelbarrows when they had been sterilised and just threw them back in the block, twelve year olds![5]

Many of the methods used were experimental and caused great suffering, even death. For instance, people were injected with diseases such as syphilis or tuberculosis, denied treatment so that the progress of the disease could be watched, and then dissected after death. Pregnant Sinti and Roma women were infected with the typhus bacteria to test the effect on their foetuses. These experiments were carried out under the guise of medical and scientific research. The most notorious perpetrator was Dr Josef Mengele, Chief Medical Officer of Auschwitz-Birkenau, who specialized in research into twins and dwarfs, the study of noma (a gangrenous condition of the mouth and face), and eye colour. Ceiji Stojka was a 10-year-old child at Birkenau. She described how her mother attempted to protect her from the studies being performed by Mengele:

> My mother didn't give them this chance. She always said to me: 'If the SS come, then don't open your eyes, look down!'

My mother had steel blue eyes and I have green eyes. And that would have been something for them! How does a Gypsy woman get green eyes? And then my mother said to me: 'You have to look away and above all—hide yourself! That's the best of all.' And it was OK like that. Otherwise I would not be here.[6]

Stojka was lucky; at least 7,000 people were experimented upon against their will. In total, the death camps, concentration camps, prison camps for Soviet POWs, and labour camps were the worst single killer in the entire war. Twelve million people died within their barbed-wire fences, including 6 million Jews.

The Perpetrators

How could one of the most civilized nations in Western Europe deliberately set out to kill all the Jews? Some argue that Hitler and other senior Nazis made a deliberate decision to kill the Jews and then carried out the plan. Hitler had long intended to 'wipe out' the Jews and the war provided him with the ideal occasion to implement his plans. In contrast, other historians believe that the Holocaust emerged from haphazard and frustrated responses to setbacks on the Eastern Front. It was the result of an 'unintentional radicalization process within the chaotic Nazi state'. A third view sees the extermination of the Jews as part of a huge plan for the racial reordering of Eastern Europe, in which the Nazis envisaged the death of 30 million Slavs. Food and supply shortages accelerated the process as Jews were killed to 'make room' for new settlers. In practice, these views are not mutually incompatible. Hitler set the tone with his virulent anti-Semitism, but he left the practical implementation to his subordinates, whose actions were often prompted by circumstances and were only gradually subsumed into a systematic, centrally directed programme of killing.

Hitler and the Nazi leaders did not act alone. One of the most disheartening results of recent research has been the realization of the widespread popular complicity in the mass murder of Jews and other groups. Indeed, the Holocaust could not have occurred without a vast array of perpetrators and bystanders. The levels of complicity in the murder infected every area of life (for instance, the property of Jews who had been deported or killed was often given to non-Jewish neighbours). 'Coercion' cannot be used as an excuse. After all, it is probably correct to claim that no one was killed for refusing to kill Jews. Furthermore, the idea that the murder of the Jews was some kind of 'bureaucratic', 'anonymous', 'mechanical', or 'industrial' affair is no longer tenable. The face-to-face nature of many instances of mass murder is undisputed. Thousands of people proved capable not simply of killing others, but of doing so in particularly sadistic ways and in front of spectators.

The perpetrators came from all classes and religious groups, and included women as well as men. Although women guards formed a small proportion of the perpetrators in the camps, the Nazi state mobilized female support to a large degree. The smooth functioning of Nazism depended upon women. Women boycotted Jewish shops and encouraged their children to join the *Hitler Jugend.* Some German women were attracted to Nazism because of its traditional approach to gender roles; others, because of its nationalist fervour, racial ideology, and anti-Communism. Popular organizations were established to harness women's support, most notably the *NSF* or *NS-Frauenschaft* (Nazi Women's Group). It is clear that most German women (and men) knew what was happening to the Jews but were largely indifferent to their fate.

It is also important to note that not all the perpetrators were Germans. Croats, Ukrainians (see Figure 17), Estonians, Latvians, Romanians, and Lithuanians were active in the killing. In many countries, local police battalions were responsible for destroying the Jewish communities. For instance, the Lithuanian Sonderkommando and the 12th Auxiliary Kommando each murdered tens of thousands of Jews. Indeed, in places like Lithuania, local fascists began attacking Jews even before the Nazi occupation. In these countries, almost the entire Jewish community was slaughtered during the war and most of these Jews were killed by people they knew in their immediate community.

The question that generates the most heated historical debates is 'why did so many people find it easy to massacre the Jews?' The list of factors enabling genocide to take place is heavily contested, but includes such things as ingrained anti-Semitism, a belief in the virtue of 'obeying orders', a desire to conform to group norms, the 'bureaucratization' of the murder process, which facilitated distancing, and an insidious brutalization in which the shock of the first murder gradually wore off, making further atrocities easier to commit. One of the most controversial explanations refers to the relative importance of ideological considerations. For some historians, the Holocaust was the result of fanatical

17 A Jewish girl being terrorized by a Ukrainian mob

anti-Semitism. The SS-General, Erich von dem Bach-Zelewski, would have agreed. He argued that 'If one preaches for years, for decades, that the Slavonic race is an inferior race, and that the Jews are no human beings at all, then it must come to such an outburst.' Blame, in this interpretation, is focused upon the entire German nation, said to be consumed by intense fear and hatred of the Jews and both willing to act and capable of acting according to their passions.

Other historians prefer to place the emphasis upon the way people became gradually accustomed to progressively brutal policies. A combination of peer pressure and moral uncertainty made people comply with the terrorist regime rather than resist and rebel. According to this explanation, such brutalization was not specific to 'Germans', but it can affect all people in the extreme circumstances of war. Given the bleak options, the decision to kill was the easiest to make. It was not the fear of punishment that made people kill, but group pressure that ensured that those who resisted killing were cast as outsiders and suffered a dramatic lowering of their esteem within the group. The perpetrators of genocide were no different from those who did not participate in the bloodletting. What distinguished them was the situation in which they found themselves. This explanation is disquieting, implying as it does that the capacity for exceptional violence lies within each of us. We are all potentially 'evil'.

Knowledge about the Holocaust

Many people turned a blind eye to the tragedy unfolding in Germany and the occupied territories. By 1942, Allied countries were aware that something terrible was taking place, but they did not pay much attention: there were too many distractions in wartime, too little time. Furthermore, from a safe distance, reports of massacres had a familiar ring: people remembered exaggerated atrocity stories from the First World War and classified these under the same heading. They could be seen as part of a long and very familiar history of pogroms and persecution of the Jews. The scale of the disaster was without precedent and could scarcely be comprehended.

In countries that did not have direct experience of Nazism, it was difficult to generate concern about the fate of persecuted groups in occupied countries. Prior to 1944, British and American soldiers had little idea of the gross brutality at the heart of Nazism and had rarely encountered any hardened Nazis. They had met only members of the *Luftwaffe*, the German Navy, and the Afrika Korps and were ignorant of the brutality of SS personnel, for example. As a consequence, people fleeing oppression faced great difficulties in getting admission to safe countries and their survival often depended upon contingent political or economic factors. For instance, the need for cheap domestic servants meant that Britain allowed 20,000 Jewish women to enter the country, while, at the same time, some trade unions were campaigning against admitting certain other groups of refugees on the grounds of putting 'our people first'.

Even inside Germany and the occupied countries, a large

proportion of Jews persisted in believing that the reports were exaggerated or that the disaster 'will not happen here or to me'. In part, their ignorance was fostered by the Nazi regime. Deception was a central part of the German arsenal. Thus, in the Netherlands, the Jewish Council of Amsterdam, led by influential Jewish figures, believed the Nazis promises of safety for the Dutch Jews and actually provided lists identifying them. Of course, by acting in this way, they hoped to prevent, or at least delay, the deportations—a naïve hope, in hindsight. In other cases, the families of deported Jews were encouraged to write to their relatives in the camps, long after the recipient was dead. A whole new euphemistic language was employed to refer to the 'special treatment' meted out to 'evacuated' Jews. Even the Jewish agency in Palestine was uncertain about what was happening. It was not until late 1942 that a group of refugees from Poland managed to convince it that the reports about the camps at Treblinka and Sobibor were true. People persisted in believing this language of denial.

Jewish Resistance

The Jews were not always led to their deaths 'like lambs to the slaughter'. From the start, there was resistance to acts of genocide. After *Kristallnacht*, for instance, the German Communist paper, *Rote Fahne* (the *Red Flag*), sported the headline: 'Against the disgrace of Jewish pogroms!' Resistance groups amongst the left wing were soon established. There are innumerable examples of 'righteous' men and women in all the occupied countries as well as in Germany who placed themselves, their families, and their entire communities at risk by helping protect the persecuted groups.

Jews also resisted. Although the first armed resistance organization was the *FPO* or the United Partisans' Organization in the Vilna Ghetto, the most famous case was the uprising in the Warsaw Ghetto in April and May 1943. The Jews of Warsaw had been confined into a ghetto that was formally sealed off from the rest of the city on 15 November 1940 by a wall. Inside, 430,000 people struggled to find enough food, shelter, and medicine to survive. The average food allocation in Warsaw was 184 calories for Jews, 669 for Poles, and 2,613 for Germans. As Göring insisted: 'If anyone goes hungry it wouldn't be the Germans.' Eighty per cent of the food in the ghetto had been smuggled in, and the most successful smugglers were children, despite the fact that the penalty was death. On 22 July 1942, forced transportation of Jews from the ghetto began. Within two months, 265,000 Jews had been taken to the death camp at Treblinka and killed. On 19 April 1943, the SS surrounded the ghetto in preparation for its complete liquidation. In response, the members of the Jewish Combat Organization (*ŻOB*) armed themselves with machine guns, rifles, and Molotov cocktails and fought back. They managed to hold out for a month against the German army. It was a bloody battle, fought building by building, hand-to-hand. At the end, although only a small number of German soldiers had perished, over 60,000 Jews were killed and, by 16 May, General Jürgen Stroop reported that 'there is no more Jewish suburb in Warsaw'. The *ŻOB* leader, 23-year-old Mordecai Anielewicz, committed suicide rather than surrender. In his last letter, written on 23 April 1943, he paid homage to 'the magnificent, heroic fighting of Jewish men in battle'. The ghetto was destroyed. One onlooker described the response of bystanders to the burning of the ghetto:

> Then came Easter Sunday . . . Mass over, the holiday crowds poured out into the sun-drenched streets. Hearts filled with Christian love, people went to look at the new unprecedented attraction that lay halfway across the city to the north, on the other side of the Ghetto wall, where Christ's Jewish brethren suffered a new and terrible Calvary not by crucifixion but by fire. What a unique spectacle! Bemused, the crowd stared at the hanging curtains of flame, listened to the roar of the conflagration, and whispered to one another, 'But the Jews— they're being roasted alive!' There was awe and relief that not they but the others had attracted the fury and vengeance of the conqueror. There was also satisfaction.[7]

Armed revolts took place in the ghettos of Krakow and Bialystok, as well, usually led by young Jews, socialists, and Communists. A small number also managed to escape and join partisan groups in the forests. Around 30,000 Jews also fought in partisan units. Acts of resistance also took place in the camps, particularly in 1943 and 1944. Jewish squads in Auschwitz, Treblinka, and Sobibor managed to create much havoc. In October 1944, the Auschwitz Fighting Group even managed to blow up Crematorium 3.

Nevertheless, escaping or resisting within the camps meant death. Mala Zimetbaum was a Jewish woman who managed to escape from Auschwitz. After being recaptured and paraded in front of the other prisoners, she suddenly began slashing her wrists with a razor, while telling the other prisoners not to be afraid. 'Their end is near,' she called, 'I am certain of this, I know. I was free.' But self-sacrifice was one thing: sacrificing the innocent was a different matter. Resistance involved one intractable moral dilemma: for every perpetrator killed or wounded, a number of hostages were murdered in reprisals. In Western Europe, ten hostages would typically be killed for every perpetrator killed by the partisans. In Eastern Europe, the ratio could be as high as 1:100. In Russia or Poland, if the resister was a Jew, 1,000 other Jews could be killed in retaliation. In the words of Auraham Tory, who found himself trapped inside the Kovno Ghetto in 1943:

> Resistance by force is meaningless. One or two Germans can be 'knocked off' but the Ghetto as a whole will bear the consequences. With just one heavy machine gun, an entire Ghetto quarter can be destroyed; 2 or 3 aircraft are enough to raze the whole Ghetto to the ground. Armed resistance is of no avail. Two or three people can escape but scores of Ghetto inmates will suffer.[8]

Freeing the Camps

Soviet troops arrived at the camps first. In July 1944, the Red Army entered Majdanek. The news of the atrocity they found was broadcast around the world. One of the first journalists to report on the camp was Roman Karman. In his words:

> In the course of my travels into liberated territory, I have never seen a more abominable sight than Majdanek near Lublin, Hitler's notorious *Vernichtungslager*, where more than half a million European men, women, and children were massacred . . . This is not a concentration camp; it is a gigantic murder plant.

That same month, the Russians liberated Belzec, Treblinka, and Sobibor. This was followed in 1945 by the liberation of Auschwitz (January), Gross Rosen (February), Stutthof (May), Sachsenhausen (April), Ravensbrück (April), and Theresienstadt (May). The British and Americans did not liberate their first major camp until April 1945. Nevertheless, in most of the camps liberated by the Russians, only the weak and the sick remained, since the Germans had evacuated the rest and marched them westwards in the notorious 'death marches'. Thousands died of exposure, hunger, and exhaustion on these marches. In this way, the Germans destroyed most of the extermination camps long before the Red Army arrived.

It was only through such waves of terror and terrorization that the Holocaust happened. The Holocaust was not inevitable, although the Jews had been demonized for centuries and by many different nationalities. All this hatred and fear converged at this one point in history to create the conditions for the worse genocide in the modern period. Nevertheless, the twisted road to genocide took many steps—discrimination, expulsion, annihilation through slave labour—before it reached outright murder.

10

Liberating Europe

Although the decisive campaign of the Second World War took place on the Eastern Front, where Soviet forces painstakingly pushed the Germans out of occupied areas, the western Allies also contributed to the German defeat by attacking from the west. German cities and towns were smashed in large-scale aerial bombardments and then, finally, in 1944, the western Allies struck in occupied France. Four years earlier, when the Allies had been humiliated and chased out of mainland Europe at Dunkirk, Churchill had defiantly told the House of Commons: 'We shall go back!' The only questions were 'when' and 'where'. Surprise was crucial, a fact the Allies were particularly conscious of after the debacle at Dieppe, when 3,658 out of the 5,100 troops—mainly Canadian—had been killed in August 1942. Operation Overlord, as it was called, simply had to succeed if Hitler was to be defeated.

Bombing Germany

The aerial campaign against Germany involved a major deployment of material and manpower but, at first, did not yield the 'knock-out blow' the Allies had hoped for. The RAF had dropped over 45,000 tons of bombs on military targets in Germany by the end of 1941, yet had made little impact on the war effort, since bombers found it difficult accurately to target entire cities, let alone specific areas. Consequently, from February 1942, British air strategy changed gear. Air Chief Marshal Arthur Harris ('Butcher Harris') became head of Bomber Command and instituted a policy of terrorization, which included incendiary raids against the ancient coastal cities of Lübeck and Rostock, followed by the 'Thousand Bomber Raid' on Cologne in May 1942. Three months later, American planes came to support the British effort. Both recognized that aerial bombardment was a key to victory. The bombing created a 'second front', it helped the USSR, and diverted Axis resources from the production of bombers and artillery to anti-aircraft guns and fighter planes.

The British and Americans were divided, however, over which *type* of bombing was most effective. Terror bombing remained a British 'sport', excused on the grounds that morale was as important as material. Harris believed that 'de-housing' German workers would damage war production as effectively as bombing war industries and docks. The fact that working-class districts were easier to hit because they were poorly defended was a further advantage of these attacks, since it reduced Allied casualties. Ironically, the inhabitants of these areas were mainly Social Democrats and

Communists, who were generally the least enthusiastic of all Germans about Hitler and 'National Socialism'. Famously, Harris was said to have replied to a policeman who pulled him over for speeding and cautioned him on the grounds that he 'could have killed someone' that 'I kill thousands of people every night'.[1] Yet the morality of terror bombing was highly questionable. Article 25 of the Hague Convention of 1907 clearly stipulated that 'the attack by Bombardment, by whatever means, of towns, villages or buildings which are undefended is prohibited' and a protocol issued by the British in 1938 and passed by the League of Nations extended Article 25 to air raids, stating that 'the intentional bombing of civilian populations is illegal. ... objectives aimed at from the air must be legitimate military targets and must be identifiable'. Some civilians in Britain and America were also uneasy. For instance, on 3 May 1943, a woman in Massachusetts wrote to the Army Air Force's Chief of Staff with the following query:

> Last month my son Ted won his wings at Randolph Field. He is now going through a bombardment school, and in a short time expects to go to the front. Will you tell me—has he become what our enemies call him, 'A Hooligan of the Air'? Is he expected to scatter death on men, women, children—to wreck churches and shrines—to be a slaughterer, not a fighting man? I remember so well when you and Frank Lahm, and Tommy Milling, won your wings. We all thought it was a new day in chivalry, bravery, manhood. What do Air Force wings mean today? In winning his wings, has Ted lost his spurs? Please tell me.[2]

In Britain, the fact that Bomber Command was virtually ignored after the war, its crew being allocated only the relatively lowly Defence Medal, suggests that there did exist a sense of unease associated with their activities. It was Harris's inability to recognize that the mass slaughter of civilians (the equivalent of attrition during the First World War) would not be enough to win the war that gave him the reputation in certain quarters of being the Douglas Haig of the Second World War, not least because death rates among bombing crews were extremely high.

By contrast, the Americans prioritized the 'precision bombing' of industrial and military targets. Morally, the Americans were in the right—but they also had greater military success. After all, as had happened when the Germans bombed British cities, the indiscriminate nature of British bombs may have caused German morale to dip, but not to crumble. Some historians even believe that terror bombing spurred on German workers and military personnel by increasing their desire to retaliate. Others argue that it caused a disintegration of the German social fabric, which was held together only by ever-more radical terror from the Nazi Party and the SS in the final stages of the war.

Nevertheless, by 1943, there was no question that the Allies were in charge of the skies. In that year, British and American air forces dropped over 200,000 tons of bombs on Germany, while the *Luftwaffe* managed to drop only 2,000 tons of bombs on Britain. The most deadly attack of 1943 was the Battle of Hamburg between late July and early August, when 50,000 civilians were killed, most in a massive firestorm (see Figure 18). One air gunner recalled: 'The raids were so terrible that one could see an entire street-map of Hamburg etched out in red fire. It was boiling and bubbling and we were shuffling incendiary bombs into this holocaust down

18 The effect of a firestorm in Hamburg, August 1943

there. I knew without doubt that if only we could keep it up we'd knock the Germans right out of the war.'[3]

By this stage, the German air force was incapable of retaliating. From the end of the Battle of Britain to the Normandy landings, German resources were forced to concentrate on the Eastern Front. Nevertheless, the Allies did not ease the pressure. Their most notorious attack was on Dresden in February 1945. The seventh largest city in Germany, Dresden had been targeted because it was an important communications centre for troops on their way to the Eastern Front. However, at the time of the bombing it was also crowded with German refugees fleeing the Soviet advance. British and American pilots found Dresden an easy target, since they were threatened by only a limited amount of flak (most had been sent to the Eastern Front, where the Russians were launching a massive offensive). Nearly 800 Allied aircraft attacked over a number of days, beginning on the night of 13 February 1945. An unusually high proportion of incendiary bombs was used (according to one estimate, three-quarters of the bombs were firebombs), creating a firestorm that spread over 8 square miles. In total, 2,640 tons of bombs were dropped and between 25,000 and 35,000 civilians were killed (although German and Russian propaganda often claimed that between 100,000 and 250,000 people were killed). In propaganda terms, the raid was a disaster, because a high proportion of those killed were refugees who had fled to Dresden in order to find safety. In a broadcast on 17 February 1945, Lord Haw-Haw (alias for William Joyce, who had fled from Britain at the beginning of the war and worked as a broadcaster in Germany) said:

> Eisenhower's headquarters have now issued a stupid and
> impudent denial of the obvious truth that the bombing of
> German towns has a terrorist motive. Churchill's spokesmen,
> both in the press and on the radio, have actually glorified in
> the air attack on Berlin and Dresden . . . Various British jour-
> nalists have written as if the murdering of German refugees
> were a first-class military achievement . . . One BBC announ-
> cer prattled, 'There is no china in Dresden today.' That was,
> perhaps, meant to be a joke: but in what sort of taste?[4]

The brutal attack on Dresden was followed by many others,
including Berlin on 3 February 1945 (killing 25,000 civilians). In total, the RAF dropped 955,000 tons of bombs on
Germany, while the USAAF dropped nearly 400,000 tons. Of
these bombs, nearly one-half of the British bombs and one-
fifth of the American bombs fell on populated areas. They
represented a new phase in the willingness of the Allies to
stretch the rules of war to allow the mass killing of civilians,
not as a *consequence* of attacking legitimate military bases but
as an end in itself. Aerial bombing represented the final
acceptance of 'total war' in the modern era and made the
subsequent bombing of Hiroshima and Nagasaki much
easier.

Operation Overlord

While Germany was being bombed into submission, the
Greater German Reich also faced attack from its western
shores. Not all the Allies agreed that the invasion of Europe
should be prioritized over the conquest of Japan. However,
the Soviet Union had been pressing for an invasion for a long

time in order to relieve the pressure it was under on the Eastern Front. Roosevelt's dictum, 'Germany first', eventually won out over Churchill's recommendation of postponement. The Allied invasion of France took place on 6 June 1944, when 156,000 troops landed in the most famous amphibious operation in the history of warfare. Allied naval and air superiority and the fact that the Germans were stretched out along a long coastline were thought to be crucial in securing victory for the Allies. Nevertheless, everyone was aware that the invasion was going to be tough. For one thing, the Germans knew that an invasion would be attempted. In addition, the Allied command was bitterly divided between General Bernard L. Montgomery and General George Patton—both egotistical military hardliners. It was to take all the skill of General Dwight D. Eisenhower, the overall coordinator, to persuade these men to work together. Rather than landing in the Pas de Calais area, which was where the English Channel was narrowest but also where the Germans expected them to land, the combined force of American, British, and Canadian units chose to land on five Normandy beaches, known as Sword, Juno, Gold, Omaha, and Utah.

For the French, the invasion was a hopeful as well as a dramatic event. Jean-Pierre Fauvel was an 18-year-old resident of Vernière-sur-Mer. He recalled:

Heavy artillery fire began about six o'clock and lasted for about an hour and the few Germans who were left in the village left very rapidly on motor bikes. Then, at about 7.30, we heard one of our neighbours shouting, 'It's the English! It's the English!' . . . By eleven o'clock most of the houses in the village, ours included, had been damaged by shelling and almost all the animals in the fields had been killed. There was

a thick smell of gunpowder in the air and there was a con-
tinual dreadful noise of guns firing, tanks and lorries going by
and all the time more and more soldiers . . . It was a beautiful
sight.[5]

German servicemen were less thrilled. At the time of the
invasion, Corporal Klaus Herrig was a 21-year-old German
radio operator, based at Le Havre. He described how all his
comrades wanted to 'get the thing over with and finished and
to go home. On the other hand, we feared for our lives, as
every soldier does, because we knew it wouldn't be fun. So I
had mixed feelings: I knew I had to do my duty as a soldier
but in my innermost heart I just hoped for it to be over.'[6]

The actual landings were traumatic for all participants.
Many beaches witnessed scenes of great carnage. One of the
worst was at Omaha, where men of the US 1st Infantry Division experienced a rough crossing that left many of them
debilitated through seasickness. Those who managed to dis-
embark successfully became the targets of expert snipers and
found themselves pinned down under the murderous fire of
an experienced German division. Nineteen-year-old John R.
Slaughter described the effect of the Omaha landing on his
comrades, noting that 'all of those who survived would be
frightened men. Some wet their britches, others cried
unashamedly, and many just had to find it within themselves
to get the job done.' Within minutes of landing, the sea was
red with blood and the screams of dying men competed with
the roar of artillery fire and MG42s.

Despite such scenes of terror, within six months the
Germans had been driven out of France and Belgium.
Within eighty days, Allied troops had reached the Seine and
the liberation of Paris—a symbolic and political necessity as

much as a military victory—was under way. The western Allies could not have achieved such results if Germany had not been fighting on two fronts. In June 1944, Germany had over 200 divisions fighting on the Eastern Front and another twenty divisions in Italy. This left Germany with only sixty divisions with which to repel the Allies on the Western Front.

The Defeat of Germany

By late 1944, much of occupied Europe had been liberated and the Allies were supremely confident that the war was nearing its end. As late as 15 December 1944, General Montgomery noted that 'the enemy is at present fighting a defensive campaign on all fronts; his situation is such that he cannot stage any major offensive operations'. How wrong he was. Within twenty-four hours, the Germans initiated what is known as the Ardennes Offensive or the Battle of the Bulge. It was Hitler's final counter-offensive in north-west Europe and was a desperate attempt to split the Allied armies in half and recapture Antwerp (a vital support port for the Allies). Taken by surprise, and with men ill-equipped to deal with the freezing conditions, the Americans and British initially faltered. The Allies were not helped by a service command crisis, as British and American leaders vied for the adoption of quite different strategies. It took the Allies five months to push back the German advance. Not only was it the largest pitched battle of the Western Front (lasting from mid-December 1944 through to January 1945); it was also Hitler's last great gamble. In the end, the Allies won because they possessed superior equipment, particularly tanks.

Mobility was the key. In only four days, the USA was able to double its infantry numbers in the Ardennes and triple its armour. Although it was America's greatest victory in Europe during the war, losses were high on all sides. In total, 20,000 men were killed and eight times that number were wounded or taken prisoner.

Defeat was a blow to the Germans. Morale dropped to an all-time low. The battle used the German reserves intended for the war with the Soviet Union and this made it easier for the USSR to consolidate its victory on the Eastern Front. As one German penned in his diary on 16 January 1945: 'four weeks ago, our attack started. How quickly everything has changed! Now everything looks hopeless.'[7] Hitler had once contemptuously called the Americans 'the Italians of the Western Alliance'—he was proved wrong.

VE Day

The war ended in stages. Officially, France was no longer at war with Germany between 1940 and 1944 and Italy left the war in 1943, although a partisan war raged for years afterwards. For most of the Allies, however, the war in Europe ended only with the death of Hitler, who was resolutely opposed to any form of surrender. It was only Hitler's suicide at the end of April 1945 that opened the way for negotiations. The war in Europe ended on 8 May 1945, when the German General Jodl signed an instrument of unconditional surrender to General Eisenhower. On 9 May 1945, German Field Marshal Keitel signed an instrument of unconditional surrender to the Russians, and the war was over in Europe, the Eastern Front, and the Balkans. In Britain, America, and many other countries, people crowded into the streets, celebrating the first hours of peace.

However, the end of the war in Europe was soured by the exposure of the concentration and death camps. People became aware of the extent of the horror in a number of different ways. In the major European cities and many towns and villages, large photographs of the atrocious conditions in the camps were set up in the central squares. In Germany itself, people were marched into cinemas to see the carnage, and groups were bussed into the camps themselves. Unrealistically, many claimed to be ignorant of the atrocities that had taken place. Perhaps, however, the ignorance and innocence of children might be accepted.

Elfie Walther, for instance, was a German schoolgirl who was sent to clean a POW camp at Sandbostel in preparation to accommodate prisoners from a nearby concentration camp. In her diary for 1 May 1945, she wrote about the process of gradually becoming aware of what had taken place. 'I am dreadfully mixed up,' she wrote. 'Can this be true? If it is as the orderlies have told us, then the pictures of Bergen-Belsen are certainly true too. And what else might there be that we have no idea of? Is this what our soldiers were fighting for? Is this what the German people have been suffering for?' She continued in her diary on the 2 May 1945: 'Why is everything so cruel? Why do they kill innocent, helpless people? One can't treat one's enemies like that! It is incomprehensible. Last night I finished with everything that I used to believe was good. People are vile pigs—all of them, including me. And is there meant to be a God?'[8]

By the end of August 1945, 90 per cent of the surviving

inmates of the camps had been repatriated, but the remaining 10 per cent were uneasy. Many had no homeland left to go to, or they were too frightened to return (particularly in the case of Polish Jews). And what did it mean to be 'liberated' if your family was dead or missing, your home and all your belongings destroyed, and you remembered how your neighbours and friends had not tried to help you? Yosef Govrin was a Romanian who had spent his childhood in ghettos and concentration camps. He recalled VE Day as the time when he first recognized the scale of the destruction:

> The destruction caused by the war and the fact that I was an orphan came home to me very forcibly on Victory Day . . . To this day, Victory Day over Nazi Germany, instead of arousing all that triumph . . . [*sic*] it was then, as a boy, that I grasped the full significance of the destruction . . . [*sic*] and really, Victory Day is engraved in my memory to this day as a day of . . . not as a day of celebration![9]

11

Hiroshima

The world war was not yet over. On VE Day, the *European Stars and Stripes* faithfully mirrored the general mood, at least amongst Allied servicemen, when its headlines declared: 'It's Over, Over Here: Six Down and Two Axis Powers to Go'. Germany, Italy, Finland, Bulgaria, Romania, and Hungary had been defeated, but Japan and Thailand remained defiant. The despair of the serviceman was illustrated in black humour in their papers (see Figure 19). The campaign that followed brought a new meaning to the expression 'modern war'. Nuclear terror signalled a new, and most frightening, shift in the ways of waging war. The bombs that destroyed Hiroshima and Nagasaki, however, were the culmination only of a terrifying aerial campaign against the people of Japan.

The Bombing Campaign in Japan

While the Soviet Union was pushing Germany out of its eastern territories and Britain and America were pushing Germany out of the countries it had occupied in the west, the

19 'Travel Orders (1945)' (cartoon by George Baker, published in *Yank*). 'Sad Sacks' was an army term for a useless soldier or a 'sad sack of shit'

conflict in the Far East continued with added fury. As in Europe, the battle from the air was crucial—and revenge was a potent motive. On 10 December 1941, an American poll revealed that 67 per cent of Americans favoured unqualified and indiscriminate bombing of Japanese cities.

The wholesale bombing of Japan began in late 1944. By July 1945, American planes had dropped more than 41,000 tons of bombs on Japanese cities, most notably in the sixty-five raids on Tokyo between December 1944 and August

1945, which resulted in 137,582 casualties. In 'Operation Meetinghouse' on 9–10 March 1945 nearly 300 B-29s raided Tokyo, destroying 20 per cent of the city's war industries and 60 per cent of its business district. Over 120,000 people died and approximately 1 million were forced to flee to the countryside. The American crews of the B-29s had to wear oxygen masks to block out the stench of burning flesh. Temperatures were so hot that people who jumped into the Simida River to flee the flames were boiled to death. Others literally had their lives sucked from them in the firestorm. As one eyewitness put it, they died 'like so many fish left gasping on the bottom of a lake that had been drained'. Japanese cities were particularly vulnerable to fire-bombing, because the buildings were made of highly flammable material, a point cruelly made in *The Times*, which noted that 'properly kindled, Japanese cities will burn like autumn leaves'.

By early August, over sixty Japanese cities had been heavily bombed, and around 600,000 people killed (see Map 4). Sixty-four per cent of the bombs dropped by the USAAF were incendiary. In the last couple of months of the war, 10 million Japanese were on the move, fleeing the cities targeted by Allied bombers. The effect was not what the Allies desired: instead of provoking large-scale demands for peace, the bombing of civilians increased Japanese anger. This was an area attack or 'terror bombing' similar to the kind conducted in Europe. Of the senior military advisers in America, only Henry L. Stimson, Secretary of War, expressed moral misgivings, pointing out that he did not want America to 'get the reputation of outdoing Hitler in atrocities'.[1]

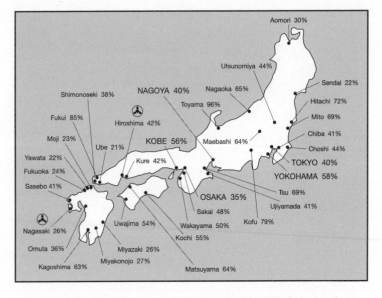

4 The percentage of Japanese cities destroyed by Allied air attack

The Atomic Bomb

6 August 1945, 8.15 a.m. It was a clear sky. The all-clear siren had just sounded when a bomb—nicknamed 'Little Boy', after Roosevelt—was dropped by parachute from ES B29 bomber, *Enola Gay.* The bomb was three metres long and weighed 3,600 kilograms. It used uranium 235 and had the power of 12.5 kilotons of TNT. It exploded 580 metres from the ground. When it ignited, the temperature of the fireball (which was 100 metres in diameter) was 1,800°C at the outer edge and 300,000°C at the centre.

Dante's Inferno had come to Hiroshima. Yamaoka Michiko, a 15-year-old girl who was 800 metres from the hypercentre of the bomb in Hiroshima, described her experiences:

> I heard the very faint sound of planes as I approached the river . . . That was the moment. There was no sound. I felt something very strong. It was terribly intense. I felt colours. It wasn't heat. You can't really say it was yellow, and it wasn't blue. At that moment I thought I would be the only one who would die. I said to myself, 'Goodbye, Mom'. They say temperatures of seven thousand degrees centigrade hit me . . . Nobody there looked like human beings. Until that moment I thought incendiary bombs had fallen. Everyone was stupefied. Humans had lost the ability to speak. People couldn't scream 'It hurts!', even when they were on fire. People didn't say 'It's hot!' They just sat catching fire. My clothes were burnt and so was my skin. I was in rags. I had braided my hair, but now it was like a lion's mane. There were people, barely breathing, trying to push their intestines back in. People with their legs wrenched off. Without heads. Or with faces burned and swollen out of shape. The scene I saw was a living hell.[2]

The walking wounded were often blind, their pupils, irises, and corneas burned out. They were vomiting blood and pus. Arms and backs were a mass of blisters. Most terrifying, they had to deal with the broiled bodies of their family, neighbours, and fellow workers. There was no precedent for such an act of war that irrevocably pushed the boundaries of limitless, technologically driven destruction.

The bomb killed approximately 140,000 people immediately. This number not does include those who died days, months, or years later—nor does it include the *pica babies* (*pica* is the Japanese word for 'flash'), who were subsequently born with abnormalities because of radiation exposure in the womb. Nor were all the victims Japanese. American prisoners of war were in the city at the time of the blast. Those POWs who survived the blast were beaten to death in the streets immediately afterwards by enraged crowds, watched by military police. Also killed were tens of thousands of Korean workers—virtual slaves in the city. Their cries for help were ignored by the Japanese.

After the bombs had been dropped, the Japanese government advised people to wear white rather than black clothes, implying that this simple measure would protect them in the event of further attack. Otherwise, the newspapers were strangely silent about the extent of the devastation. This silence was maintained until 1952: the American occupation forces forbade discussion of the bombings and ordered that all photographs be destroyed. Information about the nuclear devastation would not have predisposed the Japanese to embrace the democracy and liberalism that the American occupation forces were propagating.

Ironically, the government in Tokyo heard about the tragedy at Hiroshima from Washington DC. In a press release addressed to the American public, the release bragged about having spent $2 billion on 'the greatest scientific gamble in history—we won'. More ominously, it concluded with the words: 'we are now prepared to obliterate more rapidly and completely every productive enterprise the Japanese have above ground in any city . . . If they do not now accept our terms, they may expect a rain of ruin from the air, the like of which has never been seen on this earth.'

At the very time when Japanese leaders were debating

whether to surrender and the nature of the terms, the Americans acted again. On 9 August 1945, the B-29 *Bock's Car* dropped the second, plutonium-type bomb on Nagasaki. William Laurence flew in one of the supporting aircraft when Nagasaki was bombed. As he watched the bomb (named 'Fat Man'), his thoughts were of the elemental beauty of the explosion, rather than of the suffering it was causing. In his words:

> Awe-struck, we watched it [fire] shoot up like a meteor coming from the earth instead of from outer space, becoming ever more alive as it climbed skyward through the white clouds. It was a living thing, a new species of being, born right before our incredulous eyes ... Then ... there came shooting out of the top a giant mushroom that increased the height of the pillar to a total of 45,000 feet. The mushroom top was even more alive than the pillar, seething and boiling in a white fury of sea foam ... As the first mushroom floated off into the blue, it changed its shape into a flower-like form, its giant petal curving downward creamy white outside, rose-colored inside.

His lyricism hides a much more grotesque truth: the bomb killed around 74,000 people and left behind a legacy of radiation damage lasting for decades (see Figure 20).

Japan was in turmoil. On the same day as the atomic attack on Nagasaki, the USSR attacked Manchuria from Siberia, as it had promised to do by the Yalta Agreement of 1945, and declared war on Japan. When the Red Army attacked, it outnumbered Japanese troops by two to one. Nevertheless, the Soviet army suffered casualties of over 36,000, of which 12,000 were fatal. Thus, the Red Army made its

20 'Ground Zero', Nagasaki on the morning of 10 August 1945
(photograph by Yamahata Yosuke)

contribution to the defeat of Japan in the Asian/Pacific War. In exchange, Stalin gained a 'sphere of influence' in Manchuria, northern Korea, the Kurile Islands, and southern Sakhalin Island.

Nevertheless, some Japanese military leaders still 'held out'. The Supreme Council for the Direction of the War (known as the 'Big Six') and the Japanese Cabinet were divided. After all, they all recalled the Potsdam Proclamation, which had demanded the 'unconditional surrender of all Japanese armed forces' and insisted that

> There must be eliminated for all time the authority and influence of those who have deceived and misled the people of Japan into embarking on world conquest ... We do not intend that the Japanese be enslaved as a race or destroyed as a nation, but stern justice shall be meted out to all war criminals.

This was scarcely the language meant to reassure the Japanese that their Emperor would be retained. In the end, it was the Emperor himself who intervened, urging surrender. At noon on 15 August 1945, radios sputtered to life as, for the first time, the Emperor spoke directly to the people. He addressed his 'good and loyal subjects' in the following way:

> We declared war on America and Britain out of our sincere desire to ensure Japan's self-preservation and the stabilization of East Asia ... But now the war has lasted for nearly four years. Despite the best that has been done by everyone—the gallant fighting of our military and naval forces, the diligence and assiduity of our servants of the State and the devoted service of our 100,000,000 people—the war situation has

developed not necessarily to Japan's advantage, while the general trends of the world have all turned against her interest.

Moreover, the enemy has begun to employ a new and most cruel bomb, the power of which to do damage is, indeed, incalculable, taking the toll of many innocent lives. Should we continue to fight, it would result in an ultimate collapse and obliteration of the Japanese nation, but also it would lead to the total extinction of human civilization.

He then called on all Japanese to accept the provisions put forward for surrender. The chief opponent of surrender, the War Minister Anami, immediately concurred, declaring that 'as a Japanese soldier, I must obey my Emperor'. The day after the surrender, he committed *hara-kiri* or suicide. Japan surrendered on 14 August, with the official surrender ceremony taking place on 2 September aboard the American warship, USS *Missouri*, and presided over by General MacArthur, Supreme Commander of the Allied Powers.

Reactions to the atom bomb were diverse. For many people in the Allied countries, their main emotion was that of relief, tinged with cruel exhilaration. One of President Truman's radio broadcasts gloated over the fact that 'the Japanese began the war from the air at Pearl Harbor. They have been repaid many fold.' Truman even appealed to God, observing that the bomb was a gift from God, which 'good men' had a duty to use wisely: 'We thank God', he intoned, that 'it has come to us instead of to our enemies. May He guide us to use it in His ways and for His purpose.'[3] Less pompously, a crewman who participated in the bombing of Nagasaki penned the following words in his diary: 'Those poor Japs, but they asked for it.'[4] A poll in *Fortune* in December 1945 revealed that less than 5 per cent of Americans thought that the bomb should not have been dropped. In December 1945, two country and western singers from Kentucky recorded the first song about the bomb, entitled 'When the Atom Bomb Fell'. The song included a refrain portraying the bomb as a 'just' punishment of hell sent to torment the evil Japanese:

> Smoke and fire, it did flow through the land of Tokyo.
> There was brimstone and dust everywhere.
> When it all cleared away, there the cruel Japs did lay.
> The answer to our fighting boys' prayer.

In Washington DC, the press club prepared 'The Atomic Cocktail' (Pernod and gin) and toasted their good fortune.

Not everyone celebrated. Obviously, in Japan, there were protests. As Tokyo radio insisted: 'Such bestial tactics reveal how thin is the veneer of civilization the enemy has boasted of.' Some Americans agreed. General Dwight D. Eisenhower wondered if it had really been necessary to 'hit them with that awful thing' and the journalist Edward R. Murrow commented that 'seldom, if ever, has a war ended leaving the victors with such a sense of uncertainty and fear, with such a realization that the future is obscure and that survival is not assured'. Even the New York *Herald Tribune* found 'no satisfaction in the thought that an American aircrew had produced what must without doubt be the greatest simultaneous slaughter in the whole history of mankind', drawing a parallel between the Bomb and the 'mass butcheries of the Nazis or of the ancients'.[5]

Controversy

The dropping of the bomb remains shrouded in controversy. Three questions continue to divide commentators bitterly. First, was the decision to use the atomic bombs justified at the time? The mantra that the bomb was needed to save American lives remains the central one, particularly as articulated by ex-servicemen. Before the decision to drop the bomb, the Joint War Plans Committee told President Truman that between 25,000 and 46,000 American troops were expected to be killed in an invasion of Japan—far fewer than the 1 million lives commonly mentioned by those who defended the dropping of the bomb, and fewer than the number of Japanese civilians killed at Hiroshima and Nagasaki. Many commentators now argue that no major military expert or policy-maker at the time really believed that an invasion of the Japanese mainland would cost the Americans a million lives. This figure was a post-war myth intended to justify the dropping of the bomb on civilians.

More to the point, some evidence suggests that Japan would have surrendered if Truman had agreed to negotiate. Emperor Hirohito had attempted to petition the USA for peace on 12 July 1945. By threatening to abolish the throne of the Emperor (who was regarded as a god), the Allies crucially delayed surrender. In contrast, others argue that, even if the safety of the Emperor had been guaranteed, there was little agreement on when and how to end the war. The Japanese army command was still anxious to secure peace with honour. Finally, recent research has brought Hirohito much more than previously thought into the conduct and negotiations of the war. It is claimed that he was actively involved in planning resistance to the anticipated American invasion of Japan and was crucial in delaying peace talks. According to these historians, the claim that it was Hirohito who intervened to insist upon peace was post-war propaganda designed to protect the Emperor.

Other commentators place less emphasis upon the negotiations surrounding surrender and more on American motives and policies. They argue that the dropping of the bomb was necessary only on political grounds: it was an important weapon in the struggle between the USA and the USSR. The Americans hoped that the use of the bomb would make the USSR 'more manageable' after the war. It also meant that they would not need Soviet help in the war against Japan and thus would not have to accept Soviet influence in the region after the war. At the very least, these commentators suggest, the effect upon the Soviet Union of dropping the bomb was a 'bonus' for America.

A consideration of the necessity of using nuclear weapons must take account of the alternatives available to the Americans. Some atomic scientists argued at the time that a demonstration of the effect of the bomb would probably have been enough to persuade the already weakened Japanese to surrender (although there were fears that, if the bomb failed to 'perform satisfactorily', the demonstration might be counterproductive). Others asked: why bomb Nagasaki as well? The Allies could have continued the conventional bombing of Japanese cities, combined with the blockade. These techniques had already severely damaged Japan's economy and its ability to wage war. With the capture of Okinawa, conventional bombing could have been stepped up. The fact that many Japanese military commanders at this time were prepared to fight on—indeed, they were actively planning for 'a decisive battle at the landing point'—may have made this a less desirable alternative, particularly for American servicemen. Moreover, conventional bombing would have taken many more lives than the atomic bombs did.

The second important debate relates to the efficacy of dropping the bomb. It is indisputable that the bomb put an end to the war. But at what cost? The Japanese were already effectively defeated, having been hit hard by the sea blockade and devastated by conventional bombing raids. The Americans were accused by more cynical observers of using the bomb only to justify the $2 billion spent on the Manhattan Project (the name for the plants and test sites at Los Alamos in New Mexico, Oak Ridge in Tennessee, and Hanford in Washington, where the bomb had been developed).

Finally, was it a morally legitimate act? If the Japanese or the Germans had been the first to use the bomb, there is no question that it would have been labelled an atrocity. German scientists were indeed actively researching an atomic bomb, but they had not even approached its manufacture by April 1945. Commentators who wish to argue that dropping the bomb was a moral act insist that it saved lives—Japanese as well as American. Others go even further, arguing that in the long term the dropping of the bomb was good because, in hindsight, it was a powerful plank in nuclear deterrence. It was a 'tangible demonstration' of what we must avoid. Whatever we conclude now, the decision to use the bomb at the time did not pose any ethical problems for Truman or his administration. In effect, the nuclear bomb was dropped by default. No clear and decisive decision to drop it was ever taken; it was simply that no one intervened in a lengthy process that led to the dropping. The only concern of the politicians was how to end the war, and the bomb seemed the most effective way to do this. Indeed, except for the possibility of invading Japan, other options, such as demonstrating the devastating effect of the bomb in a deserted area or not insisting upon an unconditional surrender, were barely considered.

Yet the dropping of the atomic bombs ranks today as one of the most horrific actions of the war. Even though neither of the atomic bombs did as much damage as the conventional bombs dropped on Dresden, for example, Dresden was bombed by thousands of bombs while Hiroshima and Nagasaki were destroyed by just one bomb each. These bombs created the possibility for the first time in history that the whole world could be destroyed in one day and in one final flash of heat. The day after the bombing of Hiroshima, a *New York Times* editorial warned that 'civilization and humanity can now survive only if there is a revolution in mankind's political thinking'. Such a revolution was unlikely to take place soon.

12

Aftermath

The war was over, but entire nations were in ruins and around 55 million people were dead. On average, 20,000 people had been killed each day of the war. Many of the war leaders were also dead. Italy's Mussolini had been butchered by partisans, Joseph Goebbels and his wife had poisoned their six children and then directed an SS orderly to shoot them, and the leader of the SS, Heinrich Himmler, was to bite into a cyanide capsule on his arrest by the British. Finally, on 1 May 1945, listeners to the North German Home Service heard the following announcement: 'The German wireless broadcasts grave and important news for the German people. [Three rolls of drums.] It is reported from the Führer's headquarters that our Führer, Adolf Hitler, fighting to the last breath against Bolshevism, fell for Germany this afternoon at his operational headquarters in the Reich Chancellery.'[1] Hitler had shot himself on 30 April 1945, having first married and then poisoned his mistress, Eva Braun.

Displacement

While people crowded the streets of London and New York drinking champagne and throwing away money on what luxuries they could find, the end of the war in other European countries was welcomed with a renewed foraging for food, water, and shelter. From 1945, the roar of artillery was replaced by the quiet sufferings of millions of displaced people, service personnel, and deserters making their way 'home', wherever that might be. Indeed, the key word for the immediate post-war period was dislocation. Many had nowhere to go. In Germany, two-fifths of the population were on the move, while, in Europe as a whole, 50 million people had been driven from their homes.

The scale of demobilization was terrific. In the Far East, for instance, there were 2.2 million Japanese troops in China and Manchuria, not including the puppet troops and another 1.7 million Japanese civilians. These troops and civilians had to return home or be integrated back into their original communities. This created another kind of dislocated person. Around 160,000 Korean, Filipino, Chinese, Taiwanese, Indonesian, Dutch, and Japanese women had been forced to serve as 'comfort women' during the war. The ceaseless rapes had inflicted an awful trauma on them and now they were experiencing rejection and exclusion by their communities when they returned home after the war. Yi Yŏngsuk, a Korean 'comfort woman', described her return home:

> I didn't want to return, but I had to get on board, as all Koreans had been ordered by the government to return

home. The ship was filled with comfort women. I had no family, no relatives, and no home to go to. It would be impossible for me to find a husband. I thought it would be better to drown than to return to my country, but I didn't have the courage to throw myself overboard.[2]

Hwang Kuen Soo experienced similar emotions. She recalled how the 'comfort women' were treated 'like pigs and dogs'. Her 'life was ruined', she was 'emotionally crippled', and could never marry: 'The thought and sight of men nauseated me. I do not want compensation. What good is money? I want the truth revealed,' she insisted.[3]

Not all those who were repatriated to their 'homeland' went voluntarily. Millions of people had become displaced as they had fled from the oncoming armies of all sides, but especially from the Red Army in Eastern and Central Europe. At the Yalta Conference of February 1945, Britain, America, and the USSR had agreed to repatriate all Allied nationals after the war. The forced repatriation of many of these people back to the USSR after the war turned out to be a terrifying ordeal. Eighty-two per cent of Displaced Persons did not want to 'go home'. Jewish Displaced Persons often said things like 'Palestine is my Fatherland' or 'Poland is covered with Jewish blood; why should we call Poland home?' The fact that many of those who were forcibly repatriated had been POWs or forced labourers (after all, by the end of the war, one-third of Germany's workforce was made up of foreigners and only a tiny proportion of these workers were volunteers) was not taken into account by the Allies. Repatriation meant retribution. Ukrainians, Russians, and Byelorussians were most reluctant to be repatriated, fearing (rightly in most cases) persecution. The fear of what awaited them 'at home' increasing the further eastward they were to be sent. Thousands killed themselves rather than be sent 'home'.

Eleven million ethnic Germans were brutally expelled from Eastern Europe, or fled in fear of retribution for the crimes of Nazism. An unknown number, certainly running into hundreds of thousands, were killed or died along the way.

Finding family, friends, and loved ones haunted the Displaced Persons. Thirteen million children were without parents at the end of the war. Many of them did not know any life outside war. They were 'children without a childhood'. Who would look after them? Graffiti covered walls throughout Europe, as refugees posted photographs and names of loved ones. The names of lost children were broadcast on the radio. Other channels repeatedly recited the names of children looking for their parents. In Munich, one heavily annotated wall in a Displaced Persons' school was designated the 'Wailing Wall'.

Of all the survivors, those who came out of death or labour camps were the most pitiable. Many were so malnourished that their stomachs could not accept food and they had to be fed intravenously. Their sense of dislocation was brutal. For example, the Hungarian Miriam Steiner had been deported to Auschwitz and then Ravensbrück. She was 'liberated' by the Red Army while on a 'death march' towards Germany. Eventually, she settled in a small flat with her mother. She recalled:

> Now we began to realize the enormity of the loss, we began to understand that grandfather and grandmother and hardly

any of our relatives had returned, only that one cousin, and his father also returned later on. People said we shouldn't wait for them, but the truth is that we waited all the time for dad, and I only want to say that I often look around, as though I am still searching . . . Not for my father, it is for my brother for whom I am still looking all the time. I know it is completely unrealistic, because formally I am not searching, I cast about with my eyes.[4]

Although British and American families were spared such anguish, their transition to peacetime society was not easy, especially for families who had been interned during the war as 'enemy aliens', even though many were British or American citizens. Their scars ran deep. Most were unable to return to their former homes and jobs: they faced the difficult task of reinventing their lives with the added stigmatization of having been interned. A German American described the effect that internment had on his mother:

My mother was more bitter than my father. He could take most anything, I think. He would have been satisfied just to have a good bakery job. She thought that everything was unfair. She'd lost her house. She'd lost everything in it. It kind of broke her spirit. She'd compulsively acquire things—if she got a hold of anything she just squirreled it away. She was never really close again with some of the people as she had been, because I think the suspicion was that they were some of the people that told things to the F.B.I.[5]

Even the victorious servicemen could find returning home an alienating experience. They often felt that civilians had been unaware of what they had gone through, and were insufficiently appreciative. Such was the case of the American soldier William Manchester, who had served in the War in the

Pacific and had been severely wounded a number of times. Returning home was a humbling experience: 'It was rather diminishing to return in 1945 and discover that your own parents couldn't even pronounce the names of the islands you had conquered,' he grumbled. Many carried around their wartime hatreds all their lives. In the words of a Marine who had served in the War in the Pacific: 'To this day I haven't had a Japanese car in my garage. They say you're supposed to forgive and forget? I can't do it. I still hate them as much today as I did then.'

For all participants, however, the main conclusion to war was grief and mourning. Physical mutilation was evident everywhere, and many of the victims were young people (see Figure 21). The millions of dead had left behind even more millions of people struggling to cope with their loss. The mother of George Gill was one such person. Her son was killed in 1942 while serving with the Australian army. In a letter to her daughter, she described receiving the telegram informing her of her son's death:

> I was alone at the time and almost dressed to go into town. The cable came and as usual I hunted for my glasses, asking myself 'is it joy or sorrow', deciding it was joy ... Can you imagine the shock? We regret to inform you etc. ... I'm heart-broken and the dreadful 'never again' is more than I can bear. I feel that half my world has gone. I shouldn't say it I know, but no son could have been loved more. No need to tell you my feelings. I fear you are broken hearted too, and we are so helpless, can do nothing ... Alone, in my bed I can do as I feel and cry my heart out for him.[6]

Memories of life before the war were clung to and cherished, but nothing could heal the wound.

21 'Young War Victims, Rome 1948', showing limbless children playing (photograph by David Seymour)

Politics and Empires

The war fundamentally changed the political culture of participating nations. Respect for state authority in the occupied countries was greatly weakened. Too many leaders and civil servants had collaborated with fascist regimes. The process of reconstruction was so immense that all countries struggled to cope.

In South-East Asia, war dealt imperialism a deadly blow. Even imperial powers that were determined to retain their empires found themselves having to concede demands for independence. In August 1941, in order to secure American support for the war, Churchill had signed the Atlantic Charter, which included a promise that all inhabitants of the world would be able to identify themselves with their own government. More importantly, nationalist movements had flourished during the war, attaining a legitimacy that they had not possessed before. For many, the war had proved that 'the wisdom of the west had failed'. Within a decade of the end of the war, virtually the entire European imperial presence in Asia had been removed. One consequence of this was the contrasting treatment of people who collaborated with occupying regimes, whether German or Japanese. While many well-known European collaborators (including Pierre Laval in France, Anton Mussert in the Netherlands, and Vidkun Quisling in Norway) were executed for treason after the war, the fate of Asian collaborators was very different. Achmed Sukarno of Indonesia, Phibun Songkham in Thailand, and Manuel Roxas in the Philippines became heads of state, while Subhas Chandra Bose of India, and Bogyoke Aung San and U Ne Win of Burma became national heroes.

In Africa and India, the end of the war also signalled the end—or the beginning of the end—of imperialism. The Fifth Pan-African Congress, held in Manchester in October 1945 and attended by prominent national liberation leaders such as Kwame Nkrumah and Jomo Kenyatta, expressed the liberationist sentiments of African peoples at the end of the war. The Congress declared the right of all people to govern themselves and insisted that the colonies should be free of foreign political and economic control. This was not a message that the colonial powers welcomed. On VE Day, French police shot at 45,000 Algerians peacefully protesting against French rule. Algerian independence was not achieved until 1962 after much bloodshed. Elsewhere on the African continent, there was a resurgence of black demands for equality. The war eroded wage differentials by colour of skin, led to the growth of black trade unions, and stimulated nationalism. Unfortunately, it also began the move towards apartheid when, in 1948, the threatened white minority in South Africa voted for a government committed to apartheid policies. These were modelled on the 1935 Nuremberg Laws in Germany and imposed by white politicians who had strongly sympathized with the Nazis during the war.

Indian demands for independence were similarly stimulated during the war. Indeed, as we have seen, the desire for independence led many Indians to support the Japanese (for instance, by joining the INA) or the Germans (in the case of the India Legion). The Allies also had to contend with the Quit India movement, started by Mahatma Gandhi and the Congress Party. This had become a vast programme of civil disobedience by late 1942 and was the greatest challenge to the Raj since the Mutiny of 1857. The tragedy was that, in a compromise between the British and the various competing independence groups, India was partitioned and millions of people dislocated.

The political impact of the war was no less in Western Europe, where the defeat of Germany heralded the cold war, in which the two superpowers—the USA and the USSR—competed for world domination. By 1948, Europe was divided into two blocks. The western bloc included the western democracies and the USA, while the eastern bloc embraced the USSR, Soviet-occupied territories, and Communist states. The legacy of the Second World War was the 'iron curtain', which divided Europe into two, mutually hostile and nuclear-armed camps.

The first terrible intimation that a nuclear holocaust was a strong possibility occurred only three years after the end of the Second World War, when the Soviet Union blocked all land and water routes from West Germany across the Soviet zone of occupation into the western part of the capital city of Berlin, under Allied control. In response, the Americans and the British undertook to supply West Berliners by air in a massive operation organized by General William H. Turner, who had been instrumental in supplying Chinese forces via 'the Hump' during the Second World War. Over the following months, they flew in over 500,000 tons of food and 1.5 million tons of coal. The blockage was not lifted until 12 May 1949, when the Soviet leaders were forced to concede defeat. Eleven days after the lifting of the blockade, the Federal Republic of Germany was created out of the American, British, and French zones of occupation. The main effect of these events was a redefining of the enemy. In August, the North Atlantic Treaty Organization (NATO) was created in which non-Communist countries promised to help each other in case of foreign aggression. More generally, the attitude of the western Allies towards the Germans underwent a significant shift: the Germans in West Berlin were now able to be seen as victims rather than aggressors. The western powers' former allies—the Soviet Union—became the new threat in the post-war world.

The other great political change inspired by the war was the creation of the State of Israel in 1949. Israel absorbed around half a million Jewish victims of Nazism, becoming the physical as well as the spiritual home to Holocaust survivors. The State of Israel also became the political body responsible for submitting restitution claims on behalf of Jews. It insisted that Germany and the Soviet Union make amends for the Jewish property plundered during the war and pay for the cost of absorbing Jews into Israel. The German Democratic Republic refused to recognize the Jewish right to reparations. In contrast, in West Germany, Chancellor Konrad Adenauer as well as the opposition party, the Social Democratic Party, accepted the need for reparations and agreed to pay 3.34 billion Deutsch marks (around $845 million) between 1953 and 1965 to the State of Israel (which set aside a portion as reparations to Jewish victims of Nazism living outside Israel). Not everyone agreed that this was a good decision. Many Jews in Israel were bitterly opposed to any form of negotiation with Germany, protesting that Germany was using these talks to win political recognition from the West. Nevertheless, the reparation payments were important in the stabilization of the State of Israel.

Beyond this, many aspects of compensation and restitution remained to be settled. It was not until the very end of the twentieth century that decisions were taken to compensate former slave labourers by the German government. Homosexuals were denied compensation for their maltreatment by the Nazis because homosexual behaviour by men had been a criminal law offence long before the 'Third Reich' and continued to be for some years afterwards. Compensation to German 'Gypsies' was even decided on the advice of the same 'experts' who had identified them for imprisonment and sterilization in the first place.

Myths of Social Solidarity

In Britain and America, the main story about the aftermath of war tells of a 'good war' that promoted social solidarity and promised an end to poverty, unemployment, and sickness through state-sponsored schemes of welfare. In Britain, the 1945 election in which the Labour Party was voted into power, with 393 MPs to the Conservatives' 213, became the symbol of the new era. Certainly, the war had created a country more receptive to ideas of community welfare as opposed to Conservative individualism. The widening powers of the state were agreed to be beneficial not only in wartime but in peace as well. Trade unions were accepted as essential social partners within an enlightened capitalist system. The 'welfare state' was said to have arisen from the ashes of war. The blueprint for this state was William Beveridge's report of 1942. Throughout the land, people welcomed Beveridge's most famous statement: 'the purpose of victory is to live in a better world than the old world.'

It is easy to exaggerate the idea that the war promoted social solidarity in Britain. Indeed, many pre-war attitudes survived intact and were strengthened. The British class system barely changed. Even within air-raid shelters, social groups remained very much segregated. This was not difficult, given that less than 15 per cent of people sought refuge in public shelters or tube stations. Anyone who possessed some money used a private shelter. Looting and a thriving black market accompanied the 'Battle of Britain'. The evacuation of 1.5 million children and mothers from high-risk cities did mean that people from different parts of the country and different classes mixed more than they would normally have done, but the main result of this mixing was disgust and alienation; class hatreds remained in place. A similar story can be told about gender relations. Women's gains were transitory and limited. If anything, the war increased the prestige of manliness. Traditional sex roles were embraced with renewed fervour after the war, delaying female emancipation until the 1960s. The gulf between the classes and the sexes scarcely narrowed. Beveridge's report was a vast achievement, but from its first publication it was the scene of negotiation and compromise, as various professional groups vied for power and influence. Indeed, so-called advances (most notably the welfare state) had pre-war roots. After the chaos and years of turmoil, people longed for a return to the certainties of the past rather than for further change, however positive.

The war did not fundamentally change relations between ethnic groups in Britain either. Anti-Semitism and racial tension did not abate. In London, this was most famously revealed in the aftermath of the Bethnal Green Tube Disaster in March 1943, during which people panicked at the sound of bombs dropping in another area and, in the headlong rush to the shelter, 173 men, women, and children were crushed to death. Despite the fact that almost no Jews were involved (they avoided this shelter because it was notorious for anti-Semitic attacks), Jews were blamed for the panic. Numerous letters sent to the commission that had been set up to investigate the cause of the tragedy blamed the 'cowardly display of fear by the foreign born Jews' who 'simply lost their heads in their desire to get under shelter'. Other letters went further, demanding that the government 'Turn the dirty dogs out of the Country'.

Similarly, in America, the social-cohesion thesis ignored the great differences in consumption facilitated by the Black Market. African Americans continued to experience discrimination. The migration of large numbers of African Americans to the cities was a feature of wartime America. An estimated 700,000 Black Americans left the southern countryside for factory work in cities. Although African Americans may have gone into a wider range of jobs, they often met with hostility. The war improved the economic position of some African Americans, but prejudice and hatred remained. Although the role that African Americans played in the war was to lead to desegregation in the military by 1948, lynching continued and there were serious race riots in Tennessee, Alabama, and Pennsylvania.

Nevertheless, American society emerged from the war much stronger, and the American economy was not devastated by the war—on the contrary, it was strengthened to such an extent that, at the war's end, it dwarfed all others. The shift from isolationalism to internationalism created jobs and led to an unprecedented economic boom. Politically, there was a dramatic decline of congressional power over foreign affairs. Henceforth, the president could dictate foreign policy. American victories in the war encouraged the trend in seeing the USA as the dominant political and economic post-war power—seemingly omnipotent in military, technological, and scientific prowess. Further, post-war reconstruction resulted in a huge demand for American goods. The war achieved what Roosevelt's 'New Deal' did not: prosperity. The war turned America into a world power. In contrast, Britain changed from the world's second largest creditor to its greatest debtor.

America used its newly found economic power to influence other nations worldwide. The most important post-war initiative was launched on 5 June 1947, when the American Secretary of State, George Catlett Marshall, gave an important speech in which he expressed concern about the disintegrating economies of post-war Europe. After reminding listeners that this economic situation posed a threat to the social and political stability of these countries and, ultimately, the world, he proposed that European nations adopt a policy of reconstruction, with the help of American money. The Economic Recovery Program, better known as the Marshall Plan, emerged from this speech. Over the next four years, Congress devoted $13.3 billion to European recovery. Of course, this money was intended not only to bolster free-market economies and spur industrial and commercial reconstruction, but also to prevent the spread of Communism in Western Europe and develop trading links between Western Europe and the USA. In the longer term, it paved the way for other forms of international collaboration, including the Organization for Economic Cooperation and Development, the North Atlantic Trade Organization, and the European Union.

Destroyed Economies

Elsewhere, the war devastated economies. The USSR lost about one-third of its national wealth during the war. The campaign on the Eastern Front destroyed 70,000 Soviet villages and 1,700 Soviet towns. The Ukraine was the Soviet republic held longest by the Germans. When the Germans left in 1944, 42 per cent of all Ukrainian cities had been devastated, as well as a significant proportion of all villages. According to one estimate, the real cost of the war to the Ukraine was 1 trillion, 200 billion roubles (in 1941 prices). Arguably, no other single European country suffered so severely.

Poland was crushed. The defeat of Germany in 1945 led to the defeat of the Polish government in exile and the underground state in Poland. The subsequent domination by the USSR was greatly resented. The Polish government set out on a programme of planned reconstruction with a socialist focus. Large industry was nationalized, along with the banks and transportation systems. Land was redistributed amongst the peasantry. Linked to economic restructuring was the need to cope with massive population movements, as nearly 70,000 square miles of Polish territory had been ceded to the Soviet republics of Lithuania, Byelorussia, and the Ukraine according to the Allied agreement at Yalta and the Polish–Soviet Agreement of 16 August 1945. On the other hand, nearly 40,000 square miles of former German and Danzig territory was ceded to Poland according to the Potsdam Agreement of 20 August 1945. These changes led to massive population movements and gave the Polish government a challenge of economic integration that was formidable. Returning Polish Jews suffered most. They were generally not welcomed back. Violence frequently erupted, as in July 1946, when forty-two Jewish survivors in Kielce were killed by an angry mob.

France was also hard hit. Around 20 per cent of French homes had been destroyed. More to the point, France was no longer a world power, and its relationship with its colonies was particularly fraught. When France was occupied, its colonial territories had a number of options. Some broke away and supported the Free France movement of de Gaulle. Others, however, remained loyal to Vichy. The most important of the latter was Indochina, which allowed aircraft from its islands to sink the British battleships *Prince of Wales* and *Repulse* in December 1941. After the war, France was helped to re-establish its colonial empire, resulting in bloody conflict in Cambodia, Laos, Syria, Madagascar, Tunisia, Vietnam, and Algeria.

In Germany, 40 per cent of dwellings had been either destroyed or severely damaged in the war. There was widespread shortage of food and millions were homeless. But their main problem was coming to terms with the Nazi period. How could restitution be made for an event such as the Holocaust? In 1945, Germany was thrust back to 'zero hour' in which everything had to be rebuilt upon new foundations. Furthermore, Germany's fate was not in its own hands. The Soviet Union, Britain, France, and America each took a slice of the nation—and each brought with it its own agenda. The British and Americans wanted to re-educate the people for a democracy; France wished to annex part of Germany into the French nation; the Soviet Union wished to impose a Marxist state. They all agreed on this only: National Socialism was to be utterly purged. As we saw earlier, in 1949 the French, British, and American zones merged to become the Federal Republic of Germany while the Soviet Zone became the German Democratic Republic. Nevertheless, Allied troops (east and west) remained in occupation until reunification in 1990.

In Japan, the transition to a democratic, individualist

society after the war was not an easy one and brought with it much confusion and insecurity. In August 1945, half a million American soldiers occupied Japan and set about building the economy and society in accordance with their ideas of demilitarization and democratization. The occupation was to last until 1952 but failed to disrupt seriously the Japanese oligarchy, which, the Americans believed, was crucial in the context of the cold war fears about the threat of the Soviet Union and Communism. Japan remained a conservative, anti-Communist nation that benefited from being on the side of the Americans during the cold war. The Japanese economy quickly recovered and what became known as the Japanese 'economic miracle' was well underway by the 1950s.

Despite the process of democratization in Japan, racist attitudes towards its Asian neighbours were not extinguished. An American survey of Japanese residents in Peking in late 1945 found that 86 per cent believed that the Japanese were superior to other Far Eastern nations. Such attitudes enabled the Japanese to ignore the way they had treated other Asian peoples during the war. Also ignored were those scarred by the atomic bombs. They found themselves ostracized by Japanese society and, before 1952, had to depend upon local resources for treatment and care. Their disfigurement and psychological wounds were a curse. The genetic 'germ' in their blood made them poor marriage partners.

In Japan, one positive thing to come out of the war was the peace movement (*heiwa undo*) in 1949. This was stimulated not only by the wider discussion about what happened at Hiroshima and Nagasaki but also by cold war fears—when would World War Three begin? The peace park in Hiroshima contains a memorial upon which is inscribed a poem by Sankichi Toge, entitled 'Prelude':

> For as long as there are human beings, a world of human
>   beings,
> Bring us peace,
> Unbroken peace.[7]

War Crimes Trials

Punishing perpetrators was one of the first items on the agenda after the war. War criminals had been given plenty of warning. The St James Palace declaration of January 1942 announced that war crimes would be punished and, in October that year, Roosevelt and Churchill promised to create a United Nations War Crimes Commission. Over a year later, in November 1943, Stalin joined the British and American leaders to insist upon legal retribution. The only disagreement was over procedures. Britain favoured 'executive action'—that is, summary execution of war criminals without trial—while Roosevelt and Stalin tended to favour a trial, admitting that it would be expensive, but pointing out that summary execution would turn war criminals into martyrs and would violate 'the most fundamental principles of justice'. This was grudgingly accepted by the British. The opening remarks of Justice Robert H. Jackson at the Nuremberg Trials reflected upon this fact. In his words:

> The wrongs which we seek to condemn and punish have been so calculated, so malignant, and so devastating, that civilization cannot tolerate their being ignored because it cannot

survive their being repeated. That four great nations, flushed with victory and stung with injury, stay the hand of vengeance and voluntarily submit their captive enemies to the judgement of the law is one of the most significant tributes that power has ever paid to reason.[8]

Nevertheless, de-Nazification was not a wholehearted success. The major perpetrators who survived and did not escape to South America or elsewhere were tried at Nuremberg for crimes against humanity. The court consisted of judges and prosecutors from the four Allies: Britain, America, France, and the Soviet Union. Twenty-two influential Nazis were found guilty and were imprisoned or hanged between October 1945 and October 1946.

In the years that followed, lesser figures were prosecuted, including SS killing squads and doctors who had carried out cruel medical experiments in the camps. Most of those indicted for war crimes were Germans. In the European theatre of war, 5,556 war criminals were tried, the majority in France, America, and the United Kingdom. In 1947, the Soviet Union tried over 14,000 in the Soviet Occupied Zone of Germany alone and convicted all except 142. One of the more notable trials was of Karl Dönitz, the commander of Germany's U-boat fleet during the Battle of the Atlantic. Because of his actions during this campaign and because he succeeded Hitler as leader of the Reich on 30 April 1945, he was charged with 'waging aggressive war' and committing 'crimes against peace'. He avoided being charged with conducting unrestricted submarine warfare by the fact that the Allies had engaged in similar tactics during the War in the Pacific. This *tu quoque* ('thou also') defence caused immense embarrassment for the British and American forces. For instance, it was well known that the Chief of Naval Operations in Washington had directed Admiral Nimitz to 'execute unrestricted air and submarine warfare against Japan'. For Dönitz's crimes against peace, he served ten years in Spandau Prison.

This was not the only respect in which the Allies found themselves in a morally difficult position. After all, the Soviet judge had been the chief prosecutor in Stalin's show trials. At the trial of German war criminals at Nuremberg, Allied representatives were understandably careful in ensuring that aerial bombardment was not placed on the agenda, despite the fact that the Hague Conventions had clearly outlawed indiscriminate war on civilians. When Winston Churchill heard the news about the death sentences passed on the Nazi leaders at Nuremberg, he was alleged to have turned to General Sir Hastings Ismay and commented: 'Nuremberg shows that it's supremely important to win. You and I would be in a pretty pickle if we had not.'[9]

The problem of de-Nazification was a long-term one. Nazis who were released after serving their prison terms often regarded themselves as martyrs or as victims of 'victors' justice'. More generally, many Germans promoted an image of themselves as victims not perpetrators. Emphasis was placed on the expulsion of 11 million Germans from Eastern and Central Europe and the many thousands of German POWs who died in Soviet hands or who remained in captivity well into the 1950s. Political complicity in such denial was high. Thus, in 1949, the West German Federal Parliament passed legislation that effectively protected from prosecution 800,000 people who had participated in war crimes. Two years later, former civil servants of the Third Reich who had been barred from state service were readmitted. Pension rights were also restored. The risk of prosecution for war crimes as a result of legislation dropped dramatically and those already prosecuted had their sentences reduced. Politically, 'forgetfulness' was pursued. Chillingly, in 1949, nearly 60 per cent of Germans thought National Socialism had been 'a good idea badly carried out', while over 40 per cent still insisted that there was 'more good than evil in Nazism'. It was to be some time before this balance of opinion changed.

Elsewhere in Europe, the question of prosecuting war criminals was also difficult. In Yugoslavia, Tito's policy of 'brotherhood and unity' discouraged investigations into the killings of the war. In Lithuania, Latvia, and Estonia, a similar concern about 'national unity' reigned, despite the fact that 96 per cent of the Jews here had been killed. Prior to 1991, the responsibility for prosecuting perpetrators was in the hands of the occupying Soviets, but, after Baltic independence in 1991, these states were forced to confront their own collaboration. As late as 2000, no Nazi war criminal had been tried in these countries, and there continues to be great hostility in the Baltic states towards any such prosecution. Indeed, after German unification, SS men from Lithuania were given pensions by the Federal Republic of Germany because they had served Germany in the war. In contrast, pensions for anti-fascists were abolished on the grounds that they had served the German Democratic Republic.

In France, as elsewhere, war crimes were complicated with debates around collaboration. Liberation was accompanied by calls for collaborators to be purged from national life. Often, such calls turned into vicious practices of 'settling scores'. From September 1944, special courts were set up to try those accused of collaborating. This has left bitter wounds that remain to this day. In the early days of liberation, around 9,000 collaborators were summarily executed. Of nearly 7,000 death sentences passed by the courts, however, less than 800 were carried out. Many of those on trial were defiant. They claimed that they had been obeying a legitimate government—that of Marshal Pétain—which had been approved by the majority of the French population. They also argued that collaborationists should not be judged too harshly because, by their actions, they had prevented worse things from happening. They had practised an 'internal resistance', softening the brutal core of Nazism from within. This 'shield argument' has come under attack recently. After all, no French person could have been aware of the extent of German plans at the time of the occupation. Furthermore, the French officials went further than the Germans in deporting Jews. Indeed, many French men and women took the initiative in enacting measures against foreign Jews, sometimes against the wishes of the Germans, who initially planned to use France as a dumping ground for German Jews.

Italian war criminals were treated lightly. Many of Mussolini's former advisers returned to their jobs in the civil service. Fear of the disintegration of the state and civil service softened the purging. Thus, judges claimed that they had played a 'double game' with the fascists. The judge who had implemented the notorious racial laws ended up President of the Constitutional Court after the war. In the end, an amnesty was granted for all war crimes, except those involving 'particularly brutal torture', but the definition of 'particularly brutal torture' was broad. For instance, the Italian Supreme Court decreed that the rape of a woman partisan by a fascist military unit was not 'torture' but simply an 'insult to the honour and dignity of the woman'. On the other hand, even minor crimes committed by partisans were liable to be prosecuted with the full weight of the law.

Outside Europe, the Tokyo War Crimes Tribunal or the International Military Tribunal for the Far East was the Pacific counterpart to the Nuremberg Trials. It prosecuted twenty-eight Japanese leaders. Other war crimes trials were responsible for trying around 5,700 Japanese, Korean, and Taiwanese perpetrators. Controversially, Emperor Hirohito was given immunity from prosecution, as were many other members of the imperial family, including Hirohito's uncle, who had ordered the Japanese army to slaughter POWs at Nanking, and Hirohito's father-in-law, who had been influential in Unit 731.

Concern over the insufficiency of current law to deal with what happened during the Second World War resulted directly in the Genocide Convention of 1948 when the United Nations (which was founded as a consequence of the war) signed a convention that, for the first time, defined genocide as

> Any of the following acts committed with intent to destroy, in whole or in part, a national, ethnic, racial, or religious group, such as killing members of that group; causing serious bodily harm to members of the group; deliberately inflicting on the group conditions of life calculated to bring about its physical destruction in whole or in part; imposing measures to prevent births within the group; forcibly transferring children of the group to another group.

These acts became punishable as war crimes. The important thing to note, however, is that, owing to representations from the USSR, the Genocide Convention explicitly excluded political groups from the list of victims. This has become one of the great limiting principles of the Convention, enabling perpetrators simply to redefine their victims in political terms, as in Communist China, Cambodia, and Vietnam.

The War's Legacy

The Second World War remains crucial to much violence in the twenty-first century. Croatian wartime fascism was still used in the 1990s to justify Serbian violence. The question of Switzerland's role in hoarding Nazi gold continues to generate angry debate. The failure of Japan to apologize for atrocities carried out on American, Australian, Dutch and Chinese POWs haunts the nation. The German Nazi past can never be forgotten. 'Collaboration' is a word that strikes terror in the hearts of innumerable families all over the world. The battle over the legitimacy, or otherwise, of the dropping of two nuclear warheads continues apace, revived with particular intensity in 1995 when the Smithsonian staged its *Enola Gay* exhibition to commemorate the fiftieth anniversary of the dropping of the bomb.

At the end of the war, hundreds of millions of people were forced to sift through the ashes of their ruined lives. Loved ones were dead or 'missing' forever. Those who survived had to attempt to rebuild their lives. Their homes had been destroyed and their jobs no longer existed. Millions had been wounded. Their scars were a reminder of what they had gone through. Others suffered invisible scars. Psychological trauma would remain with them for weeks, months, years, or even decades. Survivors of the Holocaust may have been anxious to 'forget it all', but they were often tormented with survivors' guilt ('why did I survive while others did not?'), anxiety, and nightmares. The Holocaust led many religious scholars to question the view of God as omnipotent. How could God allow His chosen people to suffer in this way? Could God's voice be heard through the catastrophe? The questions of 'how' and 'why' remain with us. The question we were left with in 1945 is with us still: after the orgy of killing, after the debasement of the ethical foundations of our societies, what remains for modern culture?

13

The Memory of War

For the participants, the memory of war would always remain. Throughout this book, we have heard the voices of people who never forgot what they had experienced. For many, the search for loved ones never ended. As late as the 1980s, an old Russian woman was seen wandering the streets during the Victory Day parade with a placard around her neck reading 'Looking for Thomas Vladimirovich Kulnev, reported missing in besieged Leningrad in 1942'.[1]

Others refused to mention the war, supremely conscious of the impact that their memory could have on younger generations. In the process of 'individual memory' being transmitted and becoming 'cultural memory', the outcome could not be predicted. This was most powerfully expressed by a Hungarian Jew who had seen her entire family (including her 2-year-old daughter) killed in a death camp. In 1987 she explained why she had never mentioned her experiences to her son:

> We've never spoken about those things. It couldn't have been a constant theme, we had to live on; you couldn't forget all

> this, because you were constantly in it but to speak of it—
> would have been too much! Six of us remained alive from our
> 76-member family. You can't put that in words because if you
> lose one, that's something else but to meditate about whom I
> miss more, my child or my mother or all of them together . . .
> We only felt [in 1945–6] that you would have something to
> eat and you must live. Whether it was correct or not, I cannot
> decide, you had to live, emotionally you couldn't have been
> more ruined . . . I'm sorry I can't go on . . . If I'm going to
> speak about this, what sort of education is it for my child?
> What will I teach him against my will? Vengeance or fear?[2]

It is in this public sphere that 'memory' becomes contested.

From the time the war ended, commemoration began,
although in many different ways. In Britain, America, and
France, the end of the war was remembered as a time of
rejoicing. This was not the case for many other people. For
the Poles, Ukrainians, Balts, Chechens, Crimean Tartars,
Croats, and many people within the Soviet Union, 1944–5
was remembered as the time when one kind of tyranny was
substituted for another.

The ways in which memory of the war was transmitted were
innumerable. They included parades, days of remembrance,
literature and film, and war memorials. Some of the most
powerful war memorials are in Poland and other areas that
suffered during the campaign on the Eastern Front. In these
places, memory is often located in broken tombstones. Thus,
at Treblinka, the memorial to those killed consists of 17,000
granite shards surrounding a large obelisk broken down the
middle. Elsewhere, broken pieces of *matzevoth* (Hebrew for
tombstones) are piled in layers as a memorial to the
destruction.

In recent years, film has been one of the main ways in which the war has been remembered. The war had only just ended when the first fictionalized films began to be made, most notably the two Polish films released in 1948, *Border Street*, which focused upon the Warsaw Ghetto, and *The Last Stop*, which was filmed at Auschwitz. Documentary films have played an even larger role in changing historical images of the war. Thus, *The Sorrow and the Pity*, a French documentary released in 1970, created controversy by exposing the myth that the French had been a nation of resisters. The American docudrama *Holocaust* (1978) was similarly controversial in America, Britain, France, West Germany, and Switzerland. Although many commentators accused it of trivializing the Holocaust, the film brought the debate about the war and the Holocaust to popular attention.

The memory of the Second World War often consists of selective recitals of the past and significant silences. This is not surprising: memory itself is a battlefield, in which there are high stakes involved. The Nazis wished there to be no memory of their atrocities. As Heinrich Himmler said in October 1943, the destruction of the Jews was to be 'an unwritten and never to be written page of glory in our history'. This was one of the reasons why the Nazis built most of the camps in isolated areas and, when faced with discovery, attempted to hide the evidence. Thus, Treblinka was ploughed over and the gas chambers at Auschwitz destroyed.

But, even after the war, the prevailing urge was to engage in a very selective recital of the past. Today, many people in America, China, and South-East Asia are reluctant to visit Japan, and many Britons feel queasy about visiting Germany. In English-language histories, the memory of the Second

World War has been shaped by the cold war: after all, it is still commonplace to read histories of the war that refer to 'the Allies' as though they did not include the Soviet Union. In other nations—such as Greece, Italy, and parts of Yugoslavia—there remains a reluctance to admit that partisans and resistance fighters committed atrocities themselves. The civil war nature of the Second World War is still a sensitive topic. In the words of the Italian novelist Romano Bilenchi, 'None of us recognizes his own past.'[3]

This process of 'forgetting' is often a denial. In France, it took many decades before the role of French people in persecuting the Jews was recognized. In a typical act of denial, a 1956 documentary called *Night and Fog*, directed by Alain Resnais, was censored by the French to cut a scene showing French police collaborating with the deportations of the Jews. In other words, France reinvented itself: the Vichy regime was cordoned off in a space called 'history', while the resistance was elevated into a central place in the national identity. It was not until 1994 that a monument to the Jewish victims of Vichy was built and 16 July became a 'day of remembrance'. In Italy, a similar process of 'forgetting' took place, with the fascist past being put to one side and emphasis being placed instead on the role of Italian partisans in resisting the German occupiers from September 1943. Although the myth of resistance was particularly strong on the political left, it was also embraced by the political right (after all, it was King Victor Emmanuel who dismissed Mussolini and declared war on Germany). Dates are equally important in the Soviet Union, where memorials are generally dedicated to the 1941–5 period, denying the Nazi–Soviet Non-Aggression Pact of 1939, the invasion of Finland, and the brutal occupation of Poland. War memory in the Soviet Union is masculine, martial, and Russian, leaving little room for women, Jews, or other nationalities. Similarly, in Finland, attention has been focused on the Winter War of 1939–40 rather than the Continuation War of 1941–4 when the Finns were allies of the Germans. The one exception to this is the controversial memorial to the Opponents of Fascism in the Malmi cemetery in Helsinki. This memorial was erected in 1963 in honour of those men and women (mainly Communists) sentenced to death by the Finnish government for political reasons.

This process of denial was crucial in the nation-building process in Germany. The German Democratic Republic set aside debate about the fate of the Jews during the war, placing emphasis instead upon the valour of Soviet soldiers who had died in battle and the fate of German Communist resisters and POWs. The 3 million (or more) Soviet POWs murdered by the Germans and the millions of civilians killed had no place in German commemoration. Even Jewish sufferings were portrayed in a passive light. A similar trend is seen in West Germany, where the Nazi past was frequently relegated to 'history'. The crimes were committed 'in the name of' the Germans, as opposed to 'by' Germans. War memorials were built, but sometimes existed alongside Nazi monuments and museums. Attention was focused much more upon the *Volksdeutsch* expellees from Eastern Europe: an anti-Communist stance as well as a position that bolstered the development of a positive German national identity.

Such a selective interpretation of what happened during the war was important elsewhere. In Italy, Greece, and the USSR, the plight of the Jews during the war was subsumed under the general rubric of 'fascism against anti-fascism', making the persecution of the Jews secondary to the wider struggle against fascist domination. Such a sleight of hand delayed compensation and proper restitution. Memory is as much about forgetting as remembering.

In modern memory, the war is a political tool. As mentioned earlier, Israel itself is often regarded as a monument to the Holocaust. Memorialization of the *Shoah* has a powerful political meaning, and has been used to justify ultra-nationalist myths within Israeli society. More broadly, the trial of the SS colonel Adolf Eichmann in 1961 had a huge impact, not only because it drew the attention of young Germans to the Holocaust, but also because it politicized American Jews. The fact that the trial was followed by the Six Day War of 1967, which threatened to destroy the State of Israel, also highlighted concerns. The memory of the Holocaust—or its denial—remains a central factor in the violence within the Middle East today.

In Eastern and Western Europe, the peril of turning the war into spectacle has been threatened as memory of war is appropriated by the heritage industry. From the 1980s, former battlefields have become Meccas for tourists. If the original battlefields were built over or were on the 'wrong side' of the border, replica sites were built, using deliberately aged wood or bricks. Today, the sites of terror at Auschwitz, Majdanek, and Dachau receive around 2 million visitors each year. For some commentators, the 'memorialization industry', particularly in the context of the Holocaust, is highly questionable. The marketability of the Holocaust and its exploitation within popular culture may be a dangerous trend, reducing the Holocaust to just another—even titillating—metaphor for what is horrible. For visitors, education and entertainment have been dangerously blurred.

In the Far Eastern theatre, Japanese wartime atrocities continue to divide nations. In the 1970s, debate about the Nanking massacre erupted in a particularly bitter form and was used for political ends against the Japanese. Nanking became a symbol of Chinese unity and nationalism. Similarly, in South-East Asia, the memory of the war continues to divide communities, particularly in exacerbating racial tension between the Chinese and Malay communities.

In Japan, memory of the war has undergone significant revision in the past decades. Until the 1980s, commemoration was muted, even 'blocked out' of Japanese memory. History books in Japanese dealt with it very minimally, if at all. This changed only after 1982, when it was discovered that Japan's role in the war was seriously distorted in school textbooks. In the resulting scandal, some newspapers drew attention to the way certain phrases had been changed—thus, the phrase 'aggression in North China' became 'advance into North China'. At the same time as this uproar, revelations about Unit 731 were widely publicized. From this period, there was an increasing willingness amongst the Japanese public to admit that Japan had fought a war of aggression, even if they claimed that Japan had been forced to do so in the struggle to survive. Over 80 per cent of people surveyed in the early 1980s accepted that 'contrition was appropriate for discrimination and atrocities against Chinese and Koreans in modern history'. Despite the right-wing backlash against such attitudes, in the 1990s this translated into compensation for 'comfort women' and other slave labourers.

The one exception to the pre-1980s silence about the war in Japan refers to the atomic bombs. Within Japan (and particularly after the American occupation ended in 1952) the bomb was remembered in art, literature, and film, but most famously in the black-and-white drawings by Toshi Maruki and Iri Maruki, published in a booklet called *Pika-don* ('Flash-bang') and their five murals portraying *hibakusha*. The humanity expressed in these works of art has had a great influence in promoting peace.

Politically, however, the memory of the bomb has particular resonance for Japanese nationalists, who focus on the 'barbarism' of the bomb as a way of obscuring Japan's role as aggressor. This emphasis on the bomb enables them to characterize themselves as victims rather than aggressors in the war. Equally, in America, the memory of the bomb still touches a raw nerve. Within American texts, the bombings of Hiroshima and Nagasaki are sometimes portrayed as worthy events, preventing the mass deaths of Americans and serving as a just retribution for the 'barbaric Japanese'. This memory of the War in the Pacific prevents many Americans from seeing themselves as perpetrators of atrocious aggression.

Finally, for many people, the cultural memory of the Second World War increasingly consists of death camps and the 'industrial' murder of millions of people in gas chambers. Although it is indisputable that the gas chamber took the horror of modern warfare to new heights, it ignores the tens of millions of Jews, Chinese, Poles, East Asians, Sinti, Roma, Serbs, German communists, homosexuals, and other people slaughtered face to face, using primitive instruments, pistols, or rifles. As this book has illustrated, the striking thing about mass killing during the Second World War is that it involved an incalculable number of acts of brutality and exposed almost unimaginable levels of complicity in murder throughout the globe. Evil was not 'banal'—quite the contrary: it infused every subtle nuance of the society from which it was born. Genocidal acts were nourished within both military structures and civilian structures and, to a substantial degree, perpetrators remained immune from the law. Perpetrators rarely feared ostracism from 'their side' for their violent actions. If it is beyond comprehension to contemplate the gas chambers and the calculated mass murder of millions of Jews and non-Jews alike, it is equally unbearable to remember the acts of murderous violence carried out by 'ordinary' individuals in intimate contact with their victims.

How can the 'memory' of brutality be represented? One of the most powerful memorials to the war is the 'counter-monument' created by Jochen Gerz and Esther Gerz in Harburg, a dreary suburb in Hamburg, in 1986. In a memorializing industry that too often consists of domineering structures, this monument declares itself against fascist rigidity and against individual passivity. It is composed of a tall, hollow, aluminum shaft upon which people can write their names or graffiti based on their memory and thoughts about Nazi Germany. The shaft, however, is slowly sinking into the ground. An inscription at its base reads, in German, English, French, Russian, Hebrew, Arabic, and Turkish:

> We invite the citizens of Harburg, and visitors to the town, to add their names here to ours. In doing so, we commit ourselves to remain vigilant. As more and more names cover this 12 meter tall lead column, it will gradually be lowered into the ground. One day it will have disappeared completely, and

the site of the Harburg monument against fascism, will be empty. In the end, it is only ourselves who can rise up against injustice.[4]

The choice between forgetting and remembering is ours.

Notes

1. Introduction

1. Laurence Rees, *War of the Century: When Hitler Fought Stalin* (London: BBC Worldwide, 1999), 182.
2. A. Wieviorka, 'From Survivor to Witness: Voices from the Shoah', in Jay Winter and Emmanuel Sivan (eds.), *War and Remembrance in the Twentieth Century* (Cambridge: Cambridge University Press, 1999), 125.

2. The Declaration of War in Europe

1. Norman Ingram, *The Politics of Dissent: Pacifism in France 1919–1939* (Oxford: Clarendon Press, 1991), 3.
2. A. J. P. Taylor, *The Origins of the Second World War* (Harmondsworth: Penguin, 1979), 9.
3. Joachim Remak, *The Origins of the Second World War* (Englewood Cliffs, NJ: Prentice-Hall, 1976), 23.
4. Randall L. Schweller, *Deadly Imbalances: Tripolarity and Hitler's Strategy of World Conquest* (New York: Columbia University Press, 1998), 139.
5. Arthur Bryant (ed.), *In Search of Peace: Speeches (1937–1938) by The Right Honourable Neville Chamberlain, M.P.* (London: Hutchinson & Co., 1939), 238.
6. Laurel Holliday, *Children's Wartime Diaries: Secret Writings from the Holocaust and World War II* (London: Piatkus, 1995), 3.
7. Robert Westall, *Children of the Blitz: Memories of Wartime Childhood* (Harmondsworth: Viking, 1985), 31–2.

8. Bernard C. Nalty, *Pearl Harbor and the Pacific War* (New York: Smithmark, 1991), 20.

9. Ben-Ami Shillony, *Politics and Culture in Wartime Japan* (Oxford: Clarendon Press, 1981), 115.

10. Haruko Taya Cook and Theodore Cook, *Japan at War: An Oral History* (New York: New Press, 1992), 77.

3. Occupied Europe

1. Richard C. Lukas, 'The Polish Experience during the Holocaust', in Michael Berenbawm (ed.), *A Mosaic of Victims: Non-Jews Persecuted and Murdered by the Nazis* (New York: New York University Press, 1990), 89.

2. Alexander B. Rossino, 'Destructive Impulses: German Soldiers and the Conquest of Poland', *Holocaust and Genocide Studies*, 11/3 (Winter 1997), 355.

3. Sybil Milton, 'Non-Jewish Children in the Camps', in Berenbawm (ed.), *A Mosaic of Victims*, 151.

4. Robert J. Young, *France and the Origins of the Second World War* (Basingstoke: Macmillan Press, 1996), 128.

5. Denise Levertov, *Collected Earlier Poems 1940–1960* (New York: New Directions Books, 1957), 3.

6. Robert Westall, *Children of the Blitz: Memories of Wartime Childhood* (Harmondsworth: Viking, 1985), 116–17.

7. Louise Willmot, 'The Channel Islands', in Bob Moore (ed.), *Resistance in Western Europe* (Oxford: Berg, 2000), 78.

8. Martin Kitchen, *Nazi Germany at War* (London: Longman, 1995), 237.

9. Harry Stone, *Writing in the Shadow: Resistance Publications in Occupied Europe* (London: Frank Cass, 1996), 11.

10. Kate Johnson (ed.), *The Special Operations Executive* (London: Imperial War Museum, 1998), 199–200.

4. Battle of the Atlantic
 1. Donald Macintyre, *The Battle of the Atlantic* (London: B. T. Batsford Ltd, 1961), 12.
 2. Chris Howard Bailey, *The Battle of the Atlantic: The Corvettes and their Crew: An Oral History* (Stroud: Alan Sutton Publishing Ltd, 1994), 74.

5. War in China, Burma, and India
 1. John Israel, *Student Nationalism in China, 1927–1937* (Stanford, Calif.: Stanford University Press, 1966), 135.
 2. Dagfinn Gatu, *Toward Revolution: War, Social Change and the Chinese Communist Party in North China 1937–45* (Stockholm: Stockholm University Press, 1983), 91.
 3. Ibid. 61.
 4. Ibid. 7.
 5. David Smurthwaite (ed.), *The Forgotten War: The British Army in the Far East 1941–45* (London: National Army Museum, 1992), 59.
 6. Louise Young, *Japan's Total Empire: Manchuria and the Culture of Wartime Imperialism* (Berkeley: University of California Press, 1998), 96.
 7. http://www.aiipowmia.com/731 holocaust.html.
 8. David Andrew Schmidt, *Ianfu: The Comfort Women of the Japanese Imperial Army of the Pacific War. Broken Silence* (Lampeter: Edwin Mellen Press, 2000), 87.
 9. http://www.aiipowmia.com/731holocaust.html.
10. George Hicks, *Japan's War Memories: Amnesia or Concealment?* (Aldershot: Ashgate, 1997), 15.
11. Trevor Ling, *Buddhism, Imperialism and War: Burma and Thailand in Modern History* (London: George Allen & Unwin, 1979), 100.

12. Van Waterford, *Prisoners of the Japanese in World War II* (Jefferson, NJ: McFarland, 1994), 3.

13. Lloyd E. Eastman, *Seeds of Destruction: Nationalist China in War and Revolution, 1937–49* (Stanford, Calif.: Stanford University Press, 1984), 204.

6. War in South-East Asia and the Pacific

1. I. C. B. Dear (ed.), *The Oxford Companion to the Second World War* (Oxford: Oxford University Press, 1995), 501.

2. Mark P. Parillo, 'Burma and Southeast Asia 1941–1945', in E. Loyd Lee, *World War II in Asia and the Pacific and the War's Aftermath with General Themes* (Westport, Conn.: Greenwood Press, 1998), 90.

3. Masanobu Tsuji, *Singapore 1941–42: The Japanese Version of the Malaya Campaign of World War II*, trans. Margaret Lake (Oxford: Oxford University Press, 1988), 280.

4. Yoji Akashi, 'Japanese Cultural Policy in Malaya and Singapore, 1942–45', in Grant K. Goodman (ed.), *Japanese Cultural Policies in Southeast Asia during World War 2* (Basingstoke: Macmillan, 1991), 126.

5. Trevor Ling, *Buddhism, Imperialism and War: Burma and Thailand in Modern History* (London: George Allen & Unwin, 1979), 100.

6. Fernando J. Manalac, *Manila: Memories of World War II* (Quezon City: Giraffe Books, 1995), 31.

7. Christopher Thorne, *The Issue of War: States, Societies and the Far Eastern Conflict of 1941–45* (London: Hamilton, 1985), 155.

8. Ibid.

9. Shigeru Sato, 'Japanese Occupation: Resistance and Collaboration in Asia', in E. Loyd Lee, *World War II in*

Asia and the Pacific and the War's Aftermath with General Themes (Westport, Conn.: Greenwood Press, 1998), 122.

10. Jan A. Krancher, *The Defining Years of the Dutch East Indies, 1942–49* (Jefferson, NJ: McFarland, 1996), 218.

11. Ralph Levenberg, 'Nothing had Prepared Me for this Kind of Brutality', in R. T. King (ed.), *War Stories: Veterans Remember WWII* (Reno, Nev.: University of Nevada Press, 1995), 61.

12. Bernard A. Millot, *The Battle of Coral Sea* (London: Allan, 1974), 20.

13. Lamont Lindstrom and Geoffrey M. White, *Island Encounters: Black and White Memories of the Pacific War* (Washington: Smithsonian Institute Press, 1990), 55.

14. Ogawa Masatsugu, 'The "Green Desert" of New Guinea', in Haruko Taya Cook and Theodore Cook, *Japan at War: An Oral History* (New York: New Press, 1992), 269.

15. Craig M. Cameron, *American Samurai: Myth, Imagination and the Conduct of Battle in the First Marine Division, 1941– 1951* (Cambridge: Cambridge University Press, 1994), 115.

16. George Feifer, *Tennozan: The Battle of Okinawa and the Atomic Bomb* (New York: Ticknor & Fields, 1992), 552.

17. Cameron, *American Samurai*, 1.

18. Lindstrom and White, *Island Encounters*, 69.

7. Italy, the Balkans, and the Desert

1. Martin Gilbert, *The Churchill Papers*, ii. *Never Surrender. May 1940–December 1940* (London: Heinemann, 1994), 50.

2. Menachem Shelah, 'Genocide and Satellite Croatia during the Second World War', in Michael Berenbawm (ed.), *A Mosaic of Victims: Non-Jews Persecuted and Murdered by the Nazis* (New York: New York University Press, 1990), 74.

3. Janet Hart, *New Voices in the Nation: Women and the Greek Resistance 1941–1964* (London: Cornell University Press, 1996), 167–8.

4. Mark Mazower, *Inside Hitler's Greece: The Experience of Occupation 1941–44* (New Haven: Yale University Press, 1993), 257.

5. Gary A. Yarrington (ed.), *World War II: Personal Accounts: Pearl Harbour to V J Day* (Austin, Tex.: Lyndon Baines Johnson Foundation, 1992), 135.

6. S. W. Mitcham, *Rommel's Desert War: The Life and Death of the Afrika Korps* (New York: Stein and Day, 1992), 183.

7. Yarrington (ed.), *World War*, 203.

8. John Strawson, *The Italian Campaign* (London: Secker & Warburg, 1987), 209.

8. The Eastern Front

1. Michael Burleigh (ed.), *Confronting the Nazi Past: New Debates on Modern German History* (New York: St Martin's Press, 1996), 132.

2. Cathy Porter and Mark Jones, *Moscow in World War II* (London: Chatto & Windus, 1987), 95.

3. http://motlc.wiesenthal.com/text.x21/xr2138.html.

4. Robin Cross, *Citadel: The Battle of Kursk* (London: Michael O'Mara, 1993), 252.

5. Eugenio Corti, *Few Returned. Twenty-Eight Days on the Russian Front, Winter 1942–43*, trans. Peter Edward Levy (Columbia: University of Missouri Press, 1997), frontispiece.

6. Robert W. Thurston and Bernd Bonwetsch (eds.), *The People's War: Responses to World War II in the Soviet Union* (Urbana, Ill.: University of Illinois Press, 2000), 20.

7. Laurel Holliday, *Children's Wartime Diaries: Secret Writings from the Holocaust and World War II* (London: Piatkus, 1995), 251.

8. Jan T. Gross, *Revolution from Abroad: The Soviet Conquest of Poland's Western Ukraine and Western Belorussia* (Princeton: Princeton University Press, 1988), 35.

9. Aleksandr Solzhenitsyn, *Prussian Nights: A Narrative Poem*, trans. Robert Conquest (London: Fontana, 1978), 41.

10. Martin Gilbert, *The Day the War Ended* (London: Harper Collins Publishers, 1995), 324.

9. The Holocaust

1. Dick de Mildt, *In the Name of the People: Perpetrators of Genocide in the Reflection of their Post-War Prosecution in West Germany* (The Hague: Martinus Nijhoff Publishers, 1996), 1–2.

2. Christopher R. Browning, *Ordinary Men: Reserve Police Battalion 101 and the Final Solution in Poland* (New York: Harper Perennial, 1993), 66–7.

3. Wolfang Benz, *The Holocaust: A German Historian Examines the Genocide* (New York: Columbia University Press, 1999), 10.

4. Betty Alt and Silvia Folts, *Weeping Violins: The Gypsy Tragedy in Europe* (Kirksville, Mo.: Thomas Jefferson University Press, 1996), 55.

5. Karola Fings, Herbert Heuss, and Frank Sparing, *From 'Race Science' to the Camps. The Gypsies during the Second World War* (Hatfield: University of Hertfordshire Press, 1997), 91–5.

6. Ibid. 105.

7. Gay Block and Malka Drucker, *Rescuers: Portraits of Moral Courage in the Holocaust* (New York: Holmes & Meier, 1992), 159.

8. Rab Bennett, *Under the Shadow of the Swastika: The Moral*

Dilemmas of Resistance and Collaboration in Hitler's Europe (Basingstoke: Macmillan Press, 1999), 228.

10. Liberating Europe

1. James Parton, *'Air Force Spoken Here': General Ira Eaker and the Command of the Air* (Bethesda, Md.: Adler and Adler, 1986), 140.
2. Conrad C. Crane, *Bombs, Cities and Civilians: American Airpower Strategy in World War II* (Lawrence, Kan.: University Press of Kansas, 1993), 28.
3. Norman Longmate, *The Bombers: The RAF Offensive against Germany 1939–45* (London: Arrow, 1998), 15.
4. Ibid. 343.
5. Russell Miller, *Nothing Less than Victory: The Oral History of D-Day* (London: Penguin, 1993), 376–7.
6. Ibid. 235.
7. Danny S. Parker, *Battle of the Bulge: Hitler's Ardennes Offensive, 1944–1945* (London: Greenhill, 1991), 297.
8. Ulrike Jordan, *Conditions of Surrender: Britons and Germans Witness the End of the War* (London: I. B. Tauris, 1997), 106–7.
9. Yehudit Kleiman and Nina Springer-Aharoni, *The Anguish of Liberation: Testimonies from 1945* (Jerusalem: Yad Vashem, 1995), 40.

11. Hiroshima

1. Conrad C. Crane, *Bombs, Cities, and Civilians: American Airpower Strategy in World War II* (Lawrence, Kan.: University Press of Kansas, 1993), 135.
2. Haruko Taya Cook and Theodore Cook, *Japan at War: An Oral History* (New York: New Press, 1992), 384–5.

3. Desmond Fennell, *Uncertain Dawn: Hiroshima and the Beginning of Post-Western Civilization* (Dublin: Sanas Press, 1996), 2.

4. Conrad C. Crane, 'The Air War against Japan and the End of the War in the Pacific', in Lloyd E. Lee (ed.), *World War II in Asia and the Pacific and the War's Aftermath with General Themes* (Westport, Conn.: Greenwood Press, 1998), 107.

5. Fennell, *Uncertain Dawn*, 2.

12. Aftermath

1. Ulrike Jordan, *Conditions of Surrender: Britons and Germans Witness the End of the War* (London: I. B. Tauris, 1997), 139.

2. Yi Yongsuk, 'I Will No Longer Harbour Resentment', in Keith Howard (ed.), *True Stories of Korean Comfort Women* (London: Cassell, 1995), 56.

3. David Andrew Schmidt, *Ianfu: The Comfort Women of the Japanese Imperial Army of the Pacific War. Broken Silence* (Lampeter: Edwin Meller Press, 2000), 128–9.

4. Yehudit Kleiman and Nina Springer-Aharoni, *The Anguish of Liberation: Testimonies from 1945* (Jerusalem: Yad Vashem, 1995), 47.

5. Timothy J. Holian, *The German-Americans and World War II: An Ethnic Experience* (New York: Peter Lang, 1996), 160.

6. Joy Damousi, *The Labour of Loss: Mourning, Memory and Wartime Bereavement in Australia* (Cambridge: Cambridge University Press, 1999), 126.

7. John W. Dower, 'The Bombed: Hiroshima and Nagasaki in Japanese Memory', in Michael J. Hogan (ed.), *Hiroshima in History and Memory* (Cambridge: Cambridge University Press, 1996), 131.

8. Howard Ball, *Prosecuting War Crimes and Genocide: The*

Twentieth Century Experience (Lawrence, Kan.: University Press of Kansas, 1999), 55.

9. Stephen Harper, *Miracle of Deliverance: The Case for the Bombing of Hiroshima and Nagasaki* (London: Sidgwick & Jackson, 1985), 200.

13. The Memory of War

1. Catherine Merridale, 'War, Death and Remembrance in Soviet Russia', in Jay Winter and Emmanuel Sivan (eds.), *War and Remembrance in the Twentieth Century* (Cambridge: Cambridge University Press, 1999), 78–9.

2. Julia Szilágyi, István Cserne, Katalin Petö, and György Szöke, 'The Second and Third Generation Holocaust Survivors and their Descendants', in Randolph L. Braham, *Studies on the Holocaust in Hungary* (Boulder, Colo.: City University of New York, 1990), 250.

3. Ruth Ben-Ghiat, 'Liberation: The Italian Cinema and the Flight from the Past', in *Italy and America: Italian, American and Italian Experiences of the Liberation of the Italian Mezzogiorno* (Naples: La Città del Sole, 1997), 455.

4. James E. Young, *The Texture of Memory: Holocaust Memorials and Meaning* (New Haven: Yale University Press, 1993), 30.

Chronology

1931	Sept.	Japan invades Manchuria
1932	Jan.	Finnish–Soviet Non-Aggression Pact
	July	Nazis win 37 per cent of the vote in partly rigged German elections
	Nov.	Nazis win 33 per cent of the vote in German elections
1933	Jan.	Hitler becomes Chancellor of Germany
	Mar.	Nazis win 44 per cent of the vote in German elections
		The Enabling Act gives Hitler dictatorial powers
	Sept.	The Soviet–Italian Non-Aggression Pact is signed
1934	Aug.	Hitler assumes presidential powers after the death of President Hindenburg. He assumes the title *Führer*
1935	Sept.	Nuremberg Laws are passed
	Oct.	Italy invades Abyssinia
1936	July	The Spanish Civil War commences
	Nov.	Germany and Japan sign the Anti-Comintern Pact
1937	July	Japanese large-scale invasion of China
	Aug.	Sino-Soviet Non-Aggression Pact
	Nov.	Italy joins Germany and Japan in the Anti-Cominterm Pact
1938	Mar.	German *Anschluss* (annexation of Austria)

	Sept./Oct.	Munich crisis and German annexation of Sudetenland from Czechoslovakia
	Nov.	*Kristallnacht* pogrom
1939	Mar.	Czechoslovakia dismantled by Germany
		End of the Spanish Civil War
	Apr.	Italy invades Albania
	May	Germany and Italy sign the Pact of Steel
	Aug.	Nazi–Soviet Non-Aggression Pact signed
	Sept.	Germany invades Poland
		Britain, France, Australia, New Zealand, and Canada declare war on Germany
		Russia invades eastern Poland
	Oct.	The first 'wolf-pack' deployment of German U-boats
	Nov.	Russia invades Finland
1940	Mar.	End of the Russo-Finnish War
	Apr.	Germans overrun Denmark and land in Norway
		Himmler orders the establishment of the concentration camp at Auschwitz
	May	Churchill replaces Chamberlain as the British Prime Minister
		The Netherlands surrenders to the Germans
		Allied troops evacuated from Dunkirk
	June	Norway surrenders
		Italy enters the war, declaring war on Britain and France, and signs an armistice with Germany
		Soviet forces occupy Lithuania
		Soviet forces invade Latvia and Estonia

		France surrenders
		Charles de Gaulle becomes leader of the Free French
	July	Pétain given dictatorial powers in France
		Battle of Britain begins
	Aug.	Italian forces invade British Somaliland
		The USSR annexes the Baltic states
	Sept.	Italians attack Egypt
		Japan signs the Tripartite Pact (with Germany and Italy)
		Germany annexes Luxembourg
	Oct.	Italy attacks Greece
		British forces land on Crete
	Nov.	Hungary, Romania, and Slovakia sign the Tripartite Pact
	Dec.	Italians defeated in North Africa and ask for German help
1941	Jan.	The First Battle of Tobruk
	Feb.	Rommel arrives in Tripoli
	Mar.	Bulgaria then Yugoslavia sign the Tripartite Pact
		Allied troops land in Greece
		Roosevelt signs the Lend-Lease Bill
		Himmler orders the construction of the camp at Birkenau (Auschwitz II)
	Apr.	Germans successfully attack Yugoslavia and Greece
		Siege at Tobruk begins
		Hungarian forces invade Yugoslavia
		Germans capture Belgrade
		Greece surrenders

	British forces evacuate Greece for Crete
May	Germans land on Crete
	British forces evacuate Crete
June	Operation Barbarossa: Germany invades the Soviet Union
	Finland declares war on the Soviet Union
	Hungary declares war on the Soviet Union
	SS killing squads begin indiscriminate mass shootings of Jews in occupied Eastern Europe
July	Britain and the USSR sign a mutual assistance treaty
Sept.	German forces encircle Leningrad
	The Germans take Kiev
	First experimental gassing at Auschwitz is conducted on Soviet POWs
Oct.	German forces attack Moscow
	Lend-Lease Act is extended to the USSR
Nov.	Kursk falls to the Germans
	Berlin is bombed
	Yalta falls to the Germans
Dec.	Japanese attack Pearl Harbor
	Japanese attack the Philippines, Malaya, and Thailand
	USA and the Allies declare war on Japan
	Germany, Italy, Romania, Hungary and Bulgaria declare war on the USA
	Japan invades Burma
	First transport of Jews arrives at Chelmno death camp

1942	Jan.	The Declaration of the United Nations is signed
		Japanese invade Borneo, Dutch East Indies, New Guinea, and the Solomon Islands
		The Wannsee Conference
	Feb.	Singapore surrenders to the Japanese
		Battle of the Java Sea
	Mar.	Japanese invade Java
		Construction of the Sobibor death camp commences
		Killing begins at the Belzec death camp
		Killing of Jews by gassing begins at Belzec camp, subsequently also at Treblinka, Auschwitz, and other camps
	Apr.	Doolittle Raid on Tokyo
		Hitler assumes total power in Germany
	May	Battle of Kharkov
		Britain invades Madagascar
		Battle of the Coral Sea
		British troops retreat through Burma into India
		RAF raid on Cologne
	June	Japanese conquer Philippines
		Battle of Midway
		Japanese land on Aleutians
		Rommel enters Egypt
	July	First Battle of El Alamein
		Construction of Treblinka extermination centre begins
	Aug.	US landing on Guadalcanal

		Battle of Savo Island
		Dieppe raid
	Sept.	German forces enter Stalingrad
		Dönitz issues the Laconia Order
	Oct.	Fierce fighting in Stalingrad
		Second Battle of El Alamein
		Japanese withdraw from Guadalcanal
	Nov.	Allied landing in north-west Africa
		Germans occupy Vichy France
		Russians encircle Stalingrad
1943	Jan.	Japanese evacuate Guadalcanal
		Churchill and Roosevelt meet at Casablanca
		Allies enter Tripoli
		Armed resistance starts in the Warsaw Ghetto
	Feb.	Japanese begin evacuating Guadalcanal
		British troops enter Tunisia
		Germans surrender at Stalingrad
	Mar.	Battle of Bismarck Sea
		RAF begin Ruhr bombing
		Rommel leaves North Africa on sick leave
	May	Axis forces surrender in Tunisia
		The rising in the Warsaw Ghetto fails
		Dambusters raid
		German offensive in Yugoslavia
	June	French Committee of National Liberation established
		Düsseldorf and Cologne bombed
	July	Battle of Kursk begins
		Allied invasion of Sicily

		Allied raid on Hamburg
		Fall of Mussolini. Badoglio forms new Italian government
	Sept.	German forces occupy Rome
		Italy surrenders to the Allies
		Finland signs an armistice with the Allies
	Oct.	Italy declares war on Germany
	Nov.	Soviets take Kiev
		Berlin bombed by the RAF
		Tehrān Conference begins
	Dec.	Berlin bombed
1944	Jan.	Soviet troops enter Estonia
		Leningrad liberated
	Feb.	Allied air forces bomb Monte Cassino
	Mar.	Soviets enter Romania
		Germans occupy Hungary
		Ardeatine Caves massacre
		Nuremberg raid
	Apr.	De Gaulle assumes command of all Free France forces
		Soviets take Odessa
	May	Soviets take Sevastopol
	June	Rome liberated
		Allied landing in Normandy
		Soviet forces attack Finland
	July	Soviets take Minsk, Pinsk, Lublin, and Kvov
		Saipan liberated from the Japanese
	Aug.	Second Warsaw Uprising begins
		Liberation of Paris
	Sept.	Russian–Finnish armistice

		Allies enter Holland
	Oct.	Allies enter Greece
	Dec.	Athens is liberated and civil war begins in Greece
		Battle of the Bulge
		Hungary declares war on Germany
1945	Jan.	Warsaw falls to the Soviets
		Soviet forces liberate Auschwitz
	Feb.	Yalta Conference between Churchill, Roosevelt, and Stalin
		US troops land on Iwo Jima
		Allied firebombing of Tokyo and Dresden
	Mar.	Allied raid on Tokyo
		USA victor in Iwo Jima
	Apr.	USA troops land on Okinawa
		Death of US President Roosevelt; replaced by Truman
		Red Army attacks Berlin
		Liberation of Belsen, Buchenwald, and Dachau camps
		Parma and Verona liberated and German troops in Italy surrender
		Pétain arrested
		Mussolini killed by partisans
		Hitler commits suicide
	May	Australians take New Guinea
		Fall of Berlin
		All German forces surrender
	June	Australians recapture Borneo
	July	Los Alamos atomic test

		Potsdam declaration demands Japanese surrender
		British Prime Minister Churchill replaced by Attlee
	Aug.	Atomic bomb dropped on Hiroshima, then Nagasaki
		USSR declares war on Japan
		Polish–Soviet Agreement
		Potsdam Agreement
	Sept.	Japan surrenders
	Nov.	Nuremberg Trials begin
1948	May	The State of Israel is founded

Further Reading

Bartov, Omer, *The Eastern Front 1941–45: German Troops and the Barbarisation of Warfare* (London: Macmillan, 1985).

—— *Murder in Our Midst: The Holocaust, Industrial Killing, and Representation* (Oxford: Oxford University Press, 1996).

Bennett, Rab, *Under the Shadow of the Swastika: The Moral Dilemmas of Resistance and Collaboration in Hitler's Europe* (Basingstoke: Macmillan Press, 1999).

Browning, Christopher R., *Fateful Months*, rev. edn. (New York: Holmes & Meier, 1991).

—— *Ordinary Men: Reserve Police Battalion 101 and the Final Solution in Poland* (New York: Harper Perennial, 1993).

Burleigh, Michael (ed.), *Confronting the Nazi Past: New Debates on Modern German History* (New York: St Martin's Press, 1996).

—— *Ethics and Extermination: Reflections on Nazi Genocide* (Cambridge: Cambridge University Press, 1997).

Crane, Conrad C., *Bombs, Cities, and Civilians: American Airpower Strategy in World War II* (Lawrence, Kan.: University Press of Kansas, 1993).

Dower, John W., *War without Mercy: Race and Power in the Pacific War* (New York: Pantheon Books, 1986).

Evans, Richard J., *In Hitler's Shadow: West German Historians and the Attempt to Escape from the Nazi Past* (New York: Pantheon Books, 1989).

Fussell, Paul, *Wartime: Understanding and Behaviour in the Second World War* (Oxford: Oxford University Press, 1990).

Gorodetsky, Gabriel, *Grand Delusion. Stalin and the German Invasion of Russia* (New Haven: Yale University Press, 1999).

Gross, Jan T., *Revolution from Abroad: The Soviet Conquest of Poland's Western Ukraine and Western Belorussia* (Princeton: Princeton University Press, 1988).

—— *Neighbours: The Destruction of the Jewish Community in Jedwabne* (Princeton: Princeton University Press, 2001).

Heale, M. J., *Franklin D. Roosevelt: The New Deal and the War* (London: Routledge, 1999).

Hicks, George, *Japan's War Memories: Amnesia or Concealment?* (Aldershot: Ashgate, 1998).

Hogan, Michael J. (ed.), *Hiroshima in History and Memory* (Cambridge: Cambridge University Press, 1996).

Holian, Timothy J., *The German-Americans in World War II: An Ethnic Experience* (New York: Peter Lang, 1996).

Holliday, Laurel, *Children's Wartime Diaries: Select Writings from the Holocaust and World War II* (London: Piatkus, 1995).

Jordan, Ulrike, *Conditions of Surrender: Britons and Germans Witness the End of the War* (London: I. B. Tauris Publishers, 1997).

Kedward, H. R., *Occupied France: Collaboration and Resistance 1940–1944* (Oxford: Blackwell, 1985).

Kershaw, Ian, *Hitler 1936–1945: Nemesis* (London: Allen Lane, 2000).

King, R. T. (ed.), *War Stories: Veterans Remember World War II* (Reno, Nev.: University of Nevada, 1995).

Lee, Lloyd E. (ed.), *World War II in Asia and the Pacific and the War's Aftermath with General Themes* (Westport, Conn.: Greenwood Press, 1998).

Lindstrom, Lamont, and White, Geoffrey M., *Island Encounters: Black and White Memories of the Pacific War* (Washington: Smithsonian Institute Press, 1990).

Mazower, Mark, *Inside Hitler's Greece: The Experience of Occupation 1941–1944* (New Haven: Yale University Press, 1993).

—— *Dark Continent: Europe's Twentieth Century* (London: Allen Lane, 1998).

Merridale, Catherine, *Night of Stone: Death and Memory in Russia* (London: Granta Books, 2000).

Mildt, Dick de, *In the Name of the People: Perpetrators of Genocide in the Reflection of their Post-War Persecution in West Germany* (The Hague: Martinus Nijhoff Publishers, 1996).

Miller, Russell, *Nothing Less than Victory: The Oral History of D-Day* (London: Pimlico, 2000).

Moore, Bob (ed.), *Resistance in Western Europe* (Oxford: Berg, 2000).

Noakes, J., and Pridham, G. (eds.), *Nazism: A Documentary Reader 1919–1945*, vols. 1–3 (Exeter: University of Exeter, 1988).

Overy, Richard J., *The Air War 1939–1945* (London: Papermac, 1987).

—— *The Origins of the Second World War* (London: Longman, 1987).

—— *Why the Allies Won* (London: Pimlico, 1996).

—— *The Road to War*, rev. and updated edn. (London: Penguin Books, 1999).

Schrijvers, Peter, *The Crush of Ruin: American Combat Soldiers in Europe during World War II* (London: Macmillan Press, 1998).

Shillony, Ben-Ami, *Politics and Culture in Wartime Japan* (Oxford: Clarendon Press, 1981).

Sorge, Martin K., *The Other Price of Hitler's War: German Military and Civilian Losses Resulting from World War II* (New York: Greenwood, 1986).

Spence, Jonathan, *The Search for Modern China* (New York: Norton, 1999).

Thurston, Robert W., and Bonwetsch, Bernd (eds.), *The People's War: Responses to World War II in the Soviet Union* (Urbana, Ill.: University of Illinois Press, 2000).

Weinberg, Gerhard L., *A World at Arms: A Global History of World War II* (Cambridge: Cambridge University Press, 1994).

—— *Germany, Hitler and World War II: Essays in Modern German and World History* (Cambridge: Cambridge University Press, 1995).

Index